A

SINGER'S
COMPANION

TO THE
CHURCH YEAR

A Singer's Companion

TO THE CHURCH YEAR

Lawrence J. Johnson

The Pastoral Press
Laurel, Maryland

ISBN: 1-56929-065-2

The Pastoral Press
P.O. Box 1470
Laurel, MD 20725
1-800-976-9669 (orders only)
301-725-0990 (information)

Printed in the United States of America

In memory of my parents

INTRODUCTION

The initial liturgical reforms implemented as the fruit of Vatican II resulted in hard times for many choirs. The introduction of the vernacular rendered obsolete much of the past repertoire. Focus on the role of the assembly and its song appeared to weaken the function of the choir. Directors and members alike were challenged to re-vision themselves and their role within the liturgical celebration.

Happily (yet not without a certain modicum of pain) the challenge has been met. Choirs are alive and well in most parish communities. There is enthusiasm, dedication, and loyalty. A highly diversified repertoire is developing. Diocesan choir festivals and workshops are becoming more frequent. Choir directors are increasingly acquiring liturgical and musical skills.

This book is intended to further the diocesan and parish efforts presently being undertaken to support the role of the choir. It does so by promoting the musical, liturgical, and spiritual growth of all who, through the art of choral song, assist and support the assembly's sung prayer.

A special word of thanks is due to my wife, Marlene Winter-Johnson, for carefully reading the manuscript of this book and for her valuable suggestions.

Isaiah 63: 16-17, 19; 64: 2-7   Psalm 80: 1-2, 14-15, 17-18
1 Corinthians 1: 3-9   Mark 13:33-37

R. *Lord, make us turn to you,*
   let us see your face and we shall be saved.

Give ear, O Shepherd of Israel.
   You who are enthroned upon the cherubim, shine forth.
Stir up your might
   and come to save us!

Turn again, O God of hosts;
   look down from heaven and see;
have regard for this vine,
   the stock that your right hand has planted.

But let your hand be upon the one at your right hand,
the one whom you made strong for yourself.
Then we will never turn back from you;
   give us life, and we will call on your name.

In Psalm 80, a song of hope and optimism, the psalmist prays that the Lord's vineyard, namely, the people of Israel, be restored.

Today, the Lord tells us that we are to be watchful, to remain awake and on guard. Isaiah's plea is that God return and come down, that the people not harden their hearts and stray from the appointed path. For our part, we join the psalmist in requesting that we turn back to the Lord whose face we shall see and who will come to redeem us.

FOR THE JOURNEY

It is not easy to observe the season of Advent. The prayers, songs, and readings of the liturgy tell us to "watch," to "prepare," to "await." And yet the world on every side cries out: "It's already here." The music and festivities of Christmas have begun well before Thanksgiving Day, only to increase in momentum as December 25 approaches. Christmas concerts are given during Advent. Even many parishes celebrate their Christmas parties well in advance of the feast.

Nonetheless, we sing, we plead

with the Lord to come. If we really believe in the transforming power of music, then there is hope. The melodies of Advent have more power than "Today is the First Sunday of Advent." In their simplicity and grace the songs of Advent can empty us of our busyness so that we can peacefully and in stillness prepare ourselves for the Lord who is coming to embrace us with his wonderful love.

ADVENT WREATH

One of the most popular Advent customs, in both our churches and our homes, is that of the Advent wreath.

This tradition began in sixteenth-century Germany among the Lutherans, and it spread from them to people of other denominations. As with many of our Christmas practices, the use of the Advent wreath came to the U.S. with the German immigrants during the nineteenth century, and it was popularized among Catholics by the liturgical movement of the 1930s and 1940s.

The Advent wreath, with its progressive lighting of four candles, is a symbol of coming, the coming of the Messiah who is the light of the world, the sun of justice rising in the east.

PRAYER

Eternal God,
you are the source
of all that is good and beautiful.
Come, visit your people.
Help us so that our song of praise
may be vigorous, strong, and faith-filled.

"To those who know a little of Christian history probably the most moving of all the reflections it brings is not the thought of the great events and the well-remembered saints, but of those innumerable millions of entirely obscure faithful men and women, every one with his or her own individual hopes and fears and joys and sorrows and loves . . . They have left no slightest trace in this world, not even a name . . . Yet each of them once believed and prayed . . . Each of them worshipped at the eucharist, and found their thoughts wandering and tried again . . ." Dom Gregory Dix, *The Shape of the Liturgy* (1945).

Isaiah 40:1-5, 9-11   Psalm 85:8-9, 10-11, 12-13
2 Peter 3:8-14   Mark 1:1-8

R. *Lord, let us see your kindness*
   and grant us your salvation.

Let me hear what God the Lord will speak,
   for he will speak peace to his people.
Surely his salvation is at hand for those who fear him
   that his glory may dwell in our land.

Steadfast love and faithfulness will meet;
   righteousness and peace will kiss each other.
Faithfulness will spring up from the ground,
   and righteousness will look down from the sky.

The Lord will give what is good,
   and our land will yield its increase.
Righteousness will go before him,
   and will make a path for his steps.

Psalm 85 begins with thanksgiving for past blessings (vv. 1-3). Then the psalmist recalls the future happiness revealed by the Lord. God has already come, and yet we await a further coming.

Today's gospel begins with the evangelist citing Isaiah: "I send my messenger before you to prepare your way . . ." The messenger prepares us for God's glory and God's works on our behalf—peace, justice, truth. This is the day when the Lord will let us see "kindness," when we will experience God's "salvation."

FOR THE JOURNEY

Surely one of the most successful postconciliar ventures has been the Rite of Christian Initiation of Adults (the RCIA, as it's called). This is the name given to a series of progressive liturgies (and the book containing the texts of these services) celebrated by the community and by the candidates for baptism or full incorporation into the church. In addition to the rites themselves, there are introductions explaining how candidates and community make this journey of faith together.

The age-old wisdom of the church knows that faith is nurtured in the midst of people. A person is formed as a member of a faith community—and indeed the community itself is formed—by people sharing in a common goal, supporting one another in love and prayer, working together, enhancing the talents of others with their own gifts. . . something choir members have known for quite some time now.

"O COME, O COME, EMMANUEL"

Imagine sitting in the manuscript room of the Bibliothèque Nationale in Paris and paging through a fifteenth-century book of processional chants when—*voilà*—you come upon the earliest written source for an Advent chant whose origins have long eluded musicologists.

Well, this is precisely what happened in 1966 when Mother Thomas Moore, an English nun and chant scholar, discovered the melody for the familiar *Veni, Veni, Emmanuel* in a chant book once owned by some French Franciscan nuns. The plainsong melody appears in a somewhat strange place, i.e., with the funeral chants and carrying the text "Bone Jesu dulcis cunctis." Is this the ultimate origin of the melody? Probably we shall never know for certain.

The Latin text of this Advent song is based on the "O Antiphons" (see *Singer's Companion, Cycle C*) but has been recast in a more petitionary mode; the text for the fourth antiphon reads: "O key of David. . . You open . . . Come and deliver . . ."; the corresponding text of the *Veni, Veni* is: "O come, O key of David, come and open . . . Make safe."

> ### PRAYER
> Faithful and living God,
> you have sent your beloved son
> to lead us on the path of salvation.
> Guide our steps, direct our voices,
> so that we may never stray
> from the way of peace and love.

"Mountains and hills will sing praise before God, and all the trees of the forests will clap their hands, because the Lord and Ruler is coming into his eternal Kingdom." Second Sunday of Advent, *Breviarium Romanum*.

Isaiah 61:1-2, 10-11   Luke 1:46-48, 49-50, 53-54
1 Thessalonians 5:16-24   John 1:6-8, 19-28

R. *My soul rejoices in my God.*

My soul magnifies the Lord,
  and my spirit rejoices in God my Savior,
for he has looked with favor on
  the lowliness of his servant.
Surely, from now on all generations will call me blessed.

For the Mighty One has done great things for me,
  and holy is his name.
His mercy is for those who fear him
  from generation to generation.

He has filled the hungry with good things,
  and sent the rich away empty.
He has helped his servant Israel,
  in remembrance of his mercy.

Today's responsorial psalm is taken from the New Testament; it is the *Magnificat* sung by Mary. Some scholars suggest that this canticle (except for v. 48) may have been a Jewish-Christian hymn which well expresses Mary's sentiments on this occasion.

The readings, continuing an old tradition of the Roman Church, reflect the motif of joy. Paul says, "rejoice always," and Isaiah, whom the Lord has sent to "bring glad tidings to the lowly," himself rejoices "heartily in the Lord." The reason for Mary's joy is the reason for our joy: the "Mighty One has done great things" for us.

FOR THE JOURNEY

There was a time when the church celebrated this Sunday (it was called "Gaudete Sunday" from the first word of the Latin Introit) with special joy and signs of celebration. Today, however, the liturgical books no longer assign any special characteristics to this day; Advent is no longer divided up, as it were. The whole season is one of joyful waiting.

Yet there is a psychological benefit in attempting and experiencing things that are new. Doing so helps us mature. Challenges bring new life, hone skills, and expand horizons. It might be a new genre of music, an unfamiliar composer, a difficult technical challenge (mastering augmented fourths can be fun). It might be a piece of plainsong or of Russian chant; perhaps an unfamiliar hymn tune.

Choirs having directors that take them to unfamiliar places are fortunate indeed. They have reason to rejoice . . . and throughout the year.

THE LITANY

One of our most common forms of sung prayer is the *litany* (from the Greek word for "supplication"). A litany is a series of short petitions, made by a prayer leader, to which people make an unchanging and brief response, often in the form of an acclamation.

The litanic form originated in the fourth-century Eastern Church from where it spread to Rome. During the Middle Ages it became a favorite type of prayer, with the Litany of the Saints and the Litany of Loretto (in honor of Mary) being most popular. Today, during Mass, we have three litanies: the Lord, Have Mercy; the general intercessions; and the Lamb of God.

The major advantage of a litany is its simple form which facilitates participation. One wonders whether the "weight" or "center" of the prayer lies not in the various intentions but rather in the people's insistent and repetitious chant.

PRAYER

Lord God,
through your only Son,
conceived by the Holy Spirit and
born of the Virgin Mary,
you have fulfilled the promises
made to your people.
May our song be that of Mary,
a song of joy, peace, and wonder.

"We do not preach only one coming of Christ, but a second as well . . . The first coming was marked by patience; the second will bring the crown of a divine kingdom." Cyril of Jerusalem (315-386).

7

2 Samuel 7:1-5, 8-11, 16   Psalm 89:1-2, 3-4, 26, 28
Romans 16:25-27   Luke 1:26-38

R. *Forever I will sing the goodness of the Lord.*

I will sing of your steadfast love, O Lord, forever;
    with my mouth I will proclaim your faithfulness to
    all generations.
I declare that your steadfast love is established forever;
    your faithfulness is as firm as the heavens.

"I have made a covenant with my chosen one,
    I have sworn to my servant, David:
'I will establish your descendants forever,
    and build your throne for all generations'."

He shall cry to me, "You are my Father,
    my God and the Rock of my salvation!"
Forever will I keep my steadfast love for him,
    and my covenant with him will stand firm.

This psalm revolves around the theme of the covenant: just as God
has been faithful in the past, so God remains faithful and will come to
the people's aid today.

Luke records the annunciation to Mary, with the angel telling her
that the prophet Nathan's promise to David is now to be fulfilled: "He
will rule over the house of Jacob forever and his reign will be without
end" (Lk 1:29). The first reading gives this promise. And the psalm
continues the thought: "I have made a covenant with David." In
Christ we too are the spiritual descendants of David and thus have
reason to "sing the goodness of the Lord."

FOR THE JOURNEY

"I can't pray the way I used to
before they made all these
changes in the Mass." Every so
often we hear an older Catholic
making a remark like this. It's indeed true, you know. They can't
pray the way they used to.

Although it is all too easy to

8

disparage the past, for numerous centuries the way in which the faithful participated at Mass was far from ideal. In fact, the people, although it was good for them to attend Mass and at times were even obliged to do so, really weren't all that necessary. Only a priest (and a server) were required. Certainly the faithful were encouraged to pray, whether the rosary or various formulas from a prayer book; in time they were even urged to "follow the Mass" by using a hand missal.

Yet this was an individual venture, each person praying as best as he or she could.

Today our liturgy and our vision have changed. We come together as a people; we pray and sing and respond as a community, as the Body of Christ, as the church. The liturgy is understood as communal activity, communal prayer. It just isn't the same as it was. And who, one might ask, is responsible for all this? Could it be the Holy Spirit?

_____"LET US PROFESS OUR FAITH"_____

There was a time when choirs gloried in singing complex and sometimes operatic settings of the creed. Today, however, this profession of faith (which, by the way, is not a prayer) is made by the whole assembly and is almost always recited as best fits a declamation.

The creed we profess at Mass is a summary of faith expressed by the Councils of Nicea (325) and of Constantinople (381) as ratified by the Council of Chalcedon (451). In the east this text entered the liturgy in the sixth century. From there it spread to the west where, in 1014, it was included in the Roman Mass on all Sundays and certain feasts.

By means of the creed we respond to the word of God proclaimed in the Scriptures and to the very presence of Christ in his word.

> **PRAYER**
> Gracious and merciful God,
> you sent your Son
> to be born from the house of David.
> Help us to be mindful of your covenant
> as we sing of your steadfast love
> which embraces people everywhere.

"Advent is a season of song . . . Encourage Advent songs, both popular and liturgical. Harness your physical and spiritual powers to foster Advent thoughts and themes." Pius Parsch, *The Church's Year of Grace* (1959).

9

Isaiah 9:1-6   Psalm 96:1-2, 2-3, 11-12, 13
Titus 2:11-14   Luke 2:1-14

R. *Today is born our Savior, Christ the Lord.*

O sing to the Lord a new song;
    sing to the Lord, all the earth.
Sing to the Lord, bless his name.

Tell of his salvation from day to day,
Declare his glory among the nations,
    his marvelous works among all the peoples.

Let the heavens be glad, and let the earth rejoice;
    let the sea roar, and all that fills it;
    let the field exult, and everything in it.
Then shall all the trees of the forest sing for joy
    before the Lord.

He is coming to judge the earth.
He will judge the world with righteousness,
    and the peoples with his truth.

Psalm 96, which appears in somewhat altered form in 1 Chronicles 16:23-33, is a hymn of joy celebrating the kingship of Yahweh. It is an act of hope—the future belongs to the God who reigns over all.

The first reading, from Isaiah, speaks of God's vast and peaceful "dominion," God's kingdom, a theme echoed by the psalmist who speaks of the Lord "coming to judge the earth."

FOR THE JOURNEY

Magical powers have long been attributed to music. In ancient times the playing of the flute was believed to bring about fertility. At the trumpet blast, the walls of Jericho were brought down. The ringing of the church bells was thought to protect the people from foul weather. In the Middle Ages the Synod of Cologne (1390) forbade the singing of the responsory *Media in vita in morte sumus* unless special permission were granted since the people attributed miraculous and deadly powers to this chant.

No doubt about it, music— like all forms of art—can have wonderful effects: it can bring comfort, understanding, joy; it can excite hearts, nourish the spirit, and unite us with one another. Truly music is "magical." It possesses the magic of God.

"ADESTE FIDELES"

During the eighteenth century the city of Douay in France was a center for persecuted English Catholics. Among the exiles living there was John Francis Wade (c. 1711-1786), who was a teacher, a bookseller, and a music copyist. And this is just about all we know about him (silence always being prudent during times of religious persecution).

Today Wade is generally acknowledged as the source (author and composer) of the familiar and much-loved *Adeste Fideles.* Already in 1782 the hymn was known in England where it was sung at the Catholic chapel of the Portuguese Embassy in London (a musical center and one place in England where the Roman Catholic liturgy was permitted). In fact, the carol was so identified with the Embassy that people called it "The Portuguese Hymn." Protestant musicians were soon attracted to the tune and used it for a variety of texts.

In 1841 Frederick Oakeley (1802-1880) made an English translation (*O Come, All Ye Faithful*) of the Latin. Today the carol is sung by many religious denominations, although with various textual differences.

> ### PRAYER
> Lord God,
> the kingdom of righteousness
> has come to us
> through the birth
> of the Word made flesh.
> Awaiting his return in glory,
> we pray that the whole world
> may one day join us
> in singing praise to your name.

"This day true peace has come down to us from heaven, this day the heavens drip honey upon the whole world." Christmas Matins, *Breviarium Romanum.*

Sirach 3:2-6, 12-14   Psalm 128:1-2, 3, 4-5
Colossians 3:12-21   Matthew 2:13-15, 19-23

R. *Happy are those who fear the Lord*
   and walk in his ways.

Happy is everyone who fears the Lord,
   who walks in his ways.
You shall eat the fruit of the labor of your hands;
   you shall be happy; and it shall go well with you.

Your wife will be like a fruitful vine
   within your house;
your children will be like olive shoots
   around your table.

Thus shall the man be blessed
   who fears the Lord.
The Lord bless you from Zion.
May you see the prosperity of Jerusalem
   all the days of your life.

Today's feast is about more than the childhood of Jesus in the home of Joseph and Mary; it is about how God's family—in each of its segments and as a whole—is to behave on earth today.

Psalm 28, which celebrates the joys of domestic life, says that we will find happiness only if we "walk in the ways of the Lord." Only then shall our family life be blessed. Only then shall we, both as individuals and as a community, prosper.

FOR THE JOURNEY

It has often been noted that the Sunday assembly is both the great includer and the great leveler: it welcomes all the baptized, the rich and the poor, the powerful and the vulnerable, the saint and the sinner, the fervent and the tepid. In God's sight all are equal, all are loved, all are lovable, since all are called to be citizens of the heavenly Jerusalem. No matter what specific reason brings people to the assembly, all are searching, in one way or another, for God.

These are the folks we serve. We do not sing for the bishop or for the pastor or for our choral director. We sing for and with these people, people like ourselves with the same dreams, hopes, and fears. By doing so we, in our own small way, help bring a little bit of God into the lives of all with whom we gather.

_____ "SILENT NIGHT" _____

Most of us know the story of how Joseph Mohr (1792-1848), an assistant parish priest in the village of Oberndorf, Austria, wrote the lyrics for *Stille Nacht*, to be used at Midnight Mass in 1818. The parish organist, Franz Gruber (1787-1863), composed a melody for this text which, because the church organ had broken down, was sung with a simple guitar accompaniment. Within a few years the hymn had become quite popular in Austria and Germany.

What is perhaps less well known is that *Silent Night*—translated by John Freeman Young (1820-1885), the second Methodist bishop of Florida—took some time before attaining any popularity in the United States. Although the carol appeared in a few collections of hymns before the turn of the last century, it was not until the 1930s that its popularity began to grow, eventually becoming a hit when sung by Bing Crosby in *The Bells of St. Mary's*. Known by all, it remains one of our most simple yet most beautiful carols.

PRAYER

Lord God,
you bless us constantly
with your gifts
of beauty and love.
May we, through our song,
give back to you
what you freely share with us
in your goodness.

"This day Christ was born . . . this day the angels are singing on earth, the archangels are rejoicing; this day the just exult and sing: Glory to God in the highest, alleluia!" Christmas Vespers, *Breviarium Romanum*.

Numbers 6:22-27   Psalm 67:1-2, 4, 5, 7
Galatians 4:4-7   Luke 2:16-21

R. *May God bless us in his mercy.*

May God be gracious to us and bless us
   and make his face to shine upon us,
that your way may be known upon earth,
   your saving power among all the nations.

Let the nations be glad and sing for joy,
   for you judge the people with equity
   and guide the nations upon earth.

Let the peoples praise you, O God,
   let all the peoples praise you.
May God continue to bless us;
   let all the ends of the earth revere him.

Psalm 67 invites the *whole* world to praise God—truly an "ecumenical" psalm. All people are called upon to give thanks to God who is requested to "bless" them, namely, to extend divine favor upon them.

The psalmist speaks of God's countenance shining upon us—a figure of speech found in today's first reading which contains the priestly or Aaronic blessing. All people—being blessed by God—can, in turn, worship God.

FOR THE JOURNEY

One of the recurring motifs of the psalms is the universal nature of redemption. All nations are called to sing for joy and to give praise to God.

Our present repertory mirrors this desire of the psalmist. Here in the U.S. we sing not only the compositions of our own grow-

ing list of talented composers, but also compositions that come to us from other countries. Furthermore, many of our traditional hymns (texts and tunes) have been inherited from Germany, England, and France; they come to us from the Lutheran, Methodist, and Anglican traditions. Chants from the ecumenical community of Taizé in France continue to grow in popularity. We sing melodies from the Shakers, melodies made popular at revival meetings, folk melodies of many national origins. The musical banquet is extensive; the foods are varied.

Truly in Christ we are one. We form one choir, the choir of many peoples and nations who are united in praise.

_____ "THE FIRST NOWELL" _____

This carol comes to us from England where, first transcribed in Cornwall, it appeared (text and melody) in a carol collection published in 1833. We simply do not know how old the carol is, but the word "Nowell" seemingly comes from the Old French *nouel* (from the Latin *natalis* meaning "birthday"). Chaucer (c.1340-1400) already knew the word: "And 'Nowell' cryeth every lusty man" (*Franklin's Tale*).

It is interesting that the first published text (1823) speaks of the angel saying Nowell "to three poor shepherds" and not to "certain poor shepherds." Medieval lore knew three shepherds and even gave them names (no doubt so that they would correspond with the three magi); in the fourth play of the Chester miracle cycle the shepherds are named Harvey, Tudd, and Trowle.

It did not take long before this carol entered Roman Catholic hymnals, doing so before the end of the nineteenth century.

> **PRAYER**
> Father in heaven,
> through your Son
> you have granted us
> spiritual blessings of every kind.
> May our voices ring with joy
> as we praise you with Mary,
> who is mother to us all.

"The Church gives us Christmas not as a substitute for sanctity, others' or our own, but to enable us to taste and feel and hear and smell, even if only for a few days, the new world that began to be born when God himself was born in Bethlehem." Robert Pelton, *Circling the Sun: Meditations on Christ in Liturgy and Time* (1986).

Isaiah 60:1-6   Psalm 72:1-2, 7-8, 10-11, 12-13
Ephesians 3:2-3, 5-6   Matthew 2:1-12

R. *Lord, every nation on earth will adore you.*

Give the king your justice, O God,
    and your righteousness to a king's son.
May he judge your people with righteousness,
    and your poor with justice.

In his days may righteousness flourish
    and peace abound, until the moon is no more.
May he have dominion from sea to sea,
    and from the river to the ends of the earth.

May the kings of Tarshish and of the isles
    render him tribute,
may the kings of Sheba and Seba
    bring gifts.
May all kings fall down before him,
    all nations give him service.

For he delivers the needy when they call,
    the poor and those who have no helper.
He has pity on the weak and the needy,
    and saves the lives of the needy.

This psalm, perhaps composed for the coronation of a Jewish king, also glorifies an ideal king who for Christians is Christ the Lord. The psalmist speaks of kings from afar—Tarshish = the far west (?); Seba = Ethiopia (?)—coming and bearing gifts.

The poem mirrors today's reading from Isaiah which tells of wealth being brought from distant places to the little city Jerusalem.

FOR THE JOURNEY

Preachers have long referred to the magi as the first in a long line of sojourners who hasten to find the King of the nations.

In a sense we are indeed all magi, following a star and being strangers in a foreign land. Like these travelers of old, we do not know at what point our journey will end. But, unlike the magi, we do know where it will end—when we enter into Jerusalem, the city of light, the kingdom of God our Father. And our gifts? Perhaps our choir—like so many other choirs—has only simple and unassuming talents, but faith and love can transform them into gold, frankincense, and myrrh.

ASSEMBLY

We have often heard that the choir, although it has its own particular ministry, is part of the assembly. Yet for many of us "assembly" perhaps remains an obscure term.

The English "assembly" translates the Greek *ekklesia*, which Acts 8:1 uses to designate the local community at Jerusalem. The term was quickly applied to all who believe in Jesus Christ.

Liturgically, "assembly" is used today to describe the people who have gathered for worship. Through their coming together the church is made present in a particular place, Christ is made present, and human life is transformed through the power of the Holy Spirit.

It is by reason of baptism that we are members of the assembly. It is through the gift of music that we, as baptized members of Christ, serve the assembly.

> ### PRAYER
> God our Father,
> you have given the throne of David
> to Jesus, your Son.
> May the coming of his kingdom
> bring peace to all who love you,
> abundance to the needy,
> and blessings to all who sing your praise.

"Today the magi gaze in deep wonder at what they see: heaven on earth, earth in heaven, man in God, God in man, one whom the whole universe cannot contain, enclosed in a tiny body." Peter Chrysologus (c. 380-c. 450).

Isaiah 42:1-4, 6-7   Psalm 29:1-2, 3-4, 3, 9-10
Acts 10:34-38   Mark 1:7-11

R. *The Lord will bless his people with peace.*

Ascribe to the Lord, O heavenly beings,
    ascribe to the Lord glory and strength.
Ascribe to the Lord the glory of his name,
    worship the Lord in holy splendor.

The voice of the Lord is over the waters;
    the Lord over mighty waters.
The voice of the Lord is powerful;
    the voice of the Lord is full of majesty.

The God of glory thunders,
    and in his temple all say, "Glory!"
The Lord sits enthroned over the flood;
    the Lord sits enthroned as king forever.

In Psalm 29 the poet relates how God is revealed in the awesome majesty and power of a thunderstorm.

When Jesus was baptized in the Jordan, a voice from heaven said: "This is my beloved Son. My favor rests on him"—words related to Isaiah's "Here is my servant whom I uphold, my chosen one with whom I am pleased." Isaiah goes on to enumerate what qualities the Messiah will bring to the world; he will "bring forth justice to the nations . . . open the eyes of the blind," etc. The reading from Acts recalls that Christ's message is "the good news of peace," and it is this gift of peace which, according to the psalmist, the Lord will grant to the people.

FOR THE JOURNEY

It was Tertullian (c.160-c.220) who said that "Christians are made, not born." This life-long process of becoming a Christian ritually begins at baptism where, through water and the Holy Spirit, a person is given new life, is joined to the Body of Christ, and thus becomes a "Christian." St. Ignatius of Antioch (c.35-

c.107) said: "Let me not merely be called Christian but be found to be one."

Most of us, baptized as infants, have no recollection of the day when we were baptized. There is no "living memory" of this foundational day in our Christian lives, and so we need constant reminders of this event, e.g., holy water, renewing baptismal vows at baptism and at Easter, the sprinkling rite at Sunday Mass.

As humans we are able to sing. But it is only as baptized Christians that we can sing to the Father as members of Christ and with the voice of Christ whose Body we form.

LITTLE FISHES WITH CHRIST

Many years ago I visited a church in Holland, and within one of its side walls was located a very large aquarium containing various types of tropical fish. This was not just an architect's novel idea but a reminder of an ancient image from our religious tradition.

Early Christian art considered the fish to be a sign of Christ and of a Christian. Some believe that the symbol derives from the first letters of the phrase "Jesus Christ, Son of God, Savior," these letters in Greek forming the word for "fish," namely, *I-ch-th-y-s*.

But there is more here. In the early church the baptismal waters were to be "living waters," namely, waters full of living things (fish).

Back to the aquarium! Tertullian also wrote: "We, being little fishes, as Jesus Christ is our great Fish, begin our life in the water, and only while we abide in the water are we safe and sound." Thus the fish was used as part of the interior decoration of ancient baptismal fonts.

When we assemble for worship, we do so as baptized members of Christ who, in the words of Tertullian, is "our great Fish."

PRAYER

Lord God,
it is in Jesus that we know your glory.
Remain ever with us
so that our words and deeds and songs
may be filled with the splendor
of his saving name.

"Music is well said to be the speech of angels." Thomas Carlyle (1795-1881)

Genesis 9:8-15

Psalm 25:4-5, 6-7, 8-9

1 Peter 3:18-22

Mark 1:12-15

R. *Your ways, O Lord, are love and truth,*
   to those who keep your covenant.

Make me to know your ways, O Lord;
   teach me your paths.
Lead me in your truth, and teach me,
   for you are the God of my salvation.

Be mindful of your mercy,
   O Lord, and of your steadfast love,
   for they have been from of old.
According to your steadfast love, remember me,
   for your goodness' sake, O Lord.

Good and upright is the Lord;
   therefore he instructs the sinners in the way.
He leads the humble in what is right,
   and teaches the humble his way.

On this Sunday those preparing for baptism or for full incorporation into the church at the approaching Easter Vigil are enrolled as members of the "elect." Baptism can only bear fruit if we heed the command of Jesus to "reform our lives." And baptism, as Peter recalls, was prefigured by the waters of the flood. According to Genesis one result of this flood was the establishment of the covenant. God is faithful to this pact; and when we faithfully carry out our baptismal commitments, we discover that the ways of God are indeed the ways of "love and truth."

FOR THE JOURNEY

Today many of us will witness the catechumens officially requesting to be initiated within the approaching Easter Vigil. This scene will be repeated in parishes throughout the country as the candidates request the community's prayers and support during the weeks ahead.

A very important part of the

catechumenal process is for the candidates to meet and share with those who have already been initiated as members of the church. One must not only study the tenets of the faith; it is also necessary to experience how this faith is lived in the church's members. It is the people of the church, the community, who give birth to new members.

The same is true for us. Why not ask a Catholic friend, or a neighbor, or a teenage daughter or son to accompany you to a rehearsal? Check with your director first, but I'm sure he or she would be delighted.

_____ THE MYSTERY OF FAITH _____

Immediately after the words of institution the priest or deacon gives the invitation "Let us proclaim the mystery of faith." The whole assembly then responds in song with an acclamation.

For centuries, the phrase *mysterium fidei* occurred within Christ's words over the cup in the Roman Canon (now our Eucharistic Prayer I): ". . . this is the cup of my blood, of the new and everlasting covenant, the mystery of faith . . ." And for many years liturgical scholars debated the meaning of this phrase, but could arrive at no agreement.

The revisers of our present Order of Mass, not wishing to eliminate a traditional expression, simply made these words part of an invitation to the people: "Let us proclaim the mystery of faith." As to the phrase's meaning, perhaps some insight is found in the first acclamatory formula: "Christ has died, Christ is risen . . ." The mystery of faith is the whole divine plan. It is all that Christ has done for us.

PRAYER

Lord, our God,
you have revealed to us
your goodness and your truth
in your only-begotten Son.
Help us to be his faithful followers,
to be true servants of your people.

"The time of Lent is a time of gladness!
With radiant purity and pure love,
Filled with resplendent prayer and all good deeds,
Let us sing with joy."
From a hymn found in the *Lenten Triodion* of the Greek Church.

Genesis 22:1-2, 9, 10-13, 15-18   Psalm 116:10, 15, 16-17, 18-19
Romans 8:31-34   Mark 9:2-10

R. *I will walk in the presence of the Lord,*
   in the land of the living.

I kept my faith, even when I said,
   "I am greatly afflicted."
Precious in the sight of the Lord
   is the death of his faithful ones.

O Lord, I am your servant;
   I am your servant, the child of your serving girl.
   You have loosed my bonds.
I will offer you a thanksgiving sacrifice
   and call on the name of the Lord.

I will pay my vows to the Lord
   in the presence of all his people,
in the courts of the house of the Lord,
   in your midst, O Jerusalem.

Psalm 116 can be divided into two parts (vv. 1-9 and vv. 10-19). The poet, first recalling a past time of need, offers up heartfelt praise.

To endure times of anguish and suffering, even when these appear to come from the Lord, is a test of faith. On such occasions we join Abraham whom God commanded to sacrifice his son. Like Abraham we are never to waver in our faith. "I kept my faith, even when I said, 'I am greatly afflicted'."

FOR THE JOURNEY

Lent can be a very individual observance. In the past it was: "I'm giving up candy (or going to the movies) during Lent." Today it might be: "I'm trying to be patient with my coworkers during Lent" or "I'm going to volunteer to work one evening each week at a local food bank."

Nonetheless, we cannot simply live our own personal Lents; the season is primarily a communal observance lived and celebrated as a time of baptismal rebirth and renewal; it is a season during which the whole community prepares itself for the approaching baptism of the catechumens.

Fasting, almsgiving, and prayer have long been the church's traditional practices during these days, with prayer often being considered as the wings lifting up fasting and almsgiving to God. Just as there can be no Lent without common prayer, so we cannot celebrate Lent without common song.

THE RECESSIONAL

In most parishes a hymn or other text is sung as the clergy and other ministers leave the sanctuary after a church service. This music is called a recessional; it is the reverse image of the processional at the beginning of the celebration. In a sense the processional symbolizes the coming together of the assembly, whereas the recessional symbolizes the assembly being sent forth to carry out its mission of peace, justice, and love.

Although the Order of Mass does not call for music at this time, custom as well as our psychological make-up have led us to expect something to accompany the departure of the ministers.

Much variety is possible: a hymn sung by the assembly, or by the assembly with the choir, or by the choir alone (this is often a good place for the choir to show its mettle). At times there might be instrumental music alone or even (e.g., on Palm Sunday) silence. Perhaps the greatest pitfall is to do the same thing each Sunday.

PRAYER
God, almighty Father,
in your mercy and love
you guide us on the way
that leads to you.
Strengthen us with your grace
and make firm our voices
as we journey to your kingdom.

"There are three things which cause faith to stand firm, devotion to remain constant, and virtue to endure. They are prayer, fasting, and mercy. Prayer knocks at the door, fasting obtains, mercy receives. Prayer, mercy, and fasting: these three are one, and they give life to each other." Peter Chrysologus (c.380-c.450).

Exodus 20:1-17 or 20:1-3, 7-8, 12-17   Psalm 19:7, 8, 9, 9-10
1 Corinthians 1:22-25   John 2:13-25

R. *Lord, you have the words of everlasting life.*

The law of the Lord is perfect,
    reviving the soul;
the decrees of the Lord are sure,
    making the wise simple.

The precepts of the Lord are right,
    rejoicing the heart;
the commandment of the Lord is clear,
    enlightening the eyes.

The fear of the Lord is pure,
    enduring forever;
the ordinances of the Lord are true
    and righteous altogether.

More to be desired are they than gold,
    even much fine gold;
sweeter also than honey,
    and drippings of the honeycomb.

Psalm 19 may originally have been two separate compositions. In this second section the psalmist praises God's commandments.

A fundamental theme of the Old Testament is obedience to the Ten Commandments which—according to the spirituality of Israel—were liberating and life-giving commands. The Decalogue was seen as a positive force in the religious experience of the people. In the words of the psalmist, God's Law is "more to be desired than gold."

FOR THE JOURNEY

Thomas Merton (1915-1968), the Trappist monk who was one of our country's most popular spiritual writers, wrote a mar- velous book on the psalms, *Bread in the Wilderness* (1953), a work that grew out of his own ex- perience in chanting the psalms each day with his fellow monks at Our Lady of Gethsemani Monastery in Kentucky.

One of the many points Merton makes is that silence is needed if the heart is really to grasp the poetic language and emotion of these religious poems. Silence is needed if the Holy Spirit is to come and assist us in grasping the mystery of Christ whose voice joins ours each time we pray the psalms.

Lent is a time of intense activity for most choirs as they prepare for the Easter Triduum. Yet there is no better season than this for taking some time out to sit in the silence of a small chapel or even in a favorite armchair, with psalter in hand, to pray, to meditate, to wait, to really taste this spiritual bread given us in the wilderness.

THE CANON

Central to the liturgy of the eucharist is its consecratory prayer which begins with the dialogue "The Lord be with you . . " and concludes with the triple Amen just before the invitiation to pray the Our Father. For centuries there was only one form of this prayer in the Roman Church, and it was called the Roman Canon, from the Greek *kanon* meaning a "measuring-rod" or "rule." This prayer was the rule to be followed in celebrating the eucharistic action.

Today in the Roman Church there are a number of such prayers, and thus the term "canon" has for the most part fallen into disuse. We speak about the "eucharistic prayer," namely, the prayer par excellence whereby the church through Christ gives praise to the Creator. What used to be called the Roman Canon is now Eucharistic Prayer I.

PRAYER

Lord God,
you have sent your Son among us
as the sun of justice.
Open our eyes to the light
of your commandments;
open our hearts
to the many melodies of your Spirit.

"The soul of one who loves God always swims in joy, always keeps holiday, and is always in the mood for singing." John of the Cross (1542-1591).

2 Chronicles 36:14-17, 19-23   Psalm 137, 1-2, 3, 4-5, 6
Ephesians 2:4-10   John 3:14-21

R. *Let my tongue be silenced, if I ever forget you!*

By the rivers of Babylon—
  there we sat down and there we wept
  when we remembered Zion.
On the willows there
  we hung our harps.

For there our captors
  asked us for songs,
and our tormentors asked for mirth, saying
  "Sing us one of the songs of Zion!"

How could we sing the Lord's song
  in a foreign land?
If I forget you, O Jerusalem,
  let my right hand wither!

Let my tongue cleave to the roof of my mouth,
  if I do not remember you,
if I do not set Jerusalem
  above my highest joy.

The psalmist, reminiscing about days past when Israel was in exile, recalls that no joyful songs were sung at that time since to do so would be inconsistent with the people's memory of Jerusalem.

The history of the Old Testament is one of sin and forgiveness, the people's unfaithfulness and God's mercy. In spite of constant infidelities, God's love is always present. We—no different than the people in exile—can never forget the Lord's goodness.

FOR THE JOURNEY

"There are no good choirs or bad choirs, only good choir directors or bad choir directors."

The technical skills of a choir depend greatly on the musical and instructional abilities of its

26

director. The choir's spirit and pride reflect that of its director. The choir's love for the people it serves mirrors the director's love for the people.

Most choral directors have invested an enormous amount of time and often money into their craft. And we, as singers, profit from this, for without a skilled director, we would not be a choir, merely a group of people who enjoy singing together, a group-sing-along, as it were. Just as we appreciate an encouraging word from our director, so he or she appreciates our encouragement and support.

PROCESSIONS

Processions, whether within or without the church building, have long been part of liturgical and devotional life. At times they are functional (getting from one place to another); at other times they are more ceremonial (starting and ending at the same place, namely, processing for the sake of processing).

People who reflect on these things remind us that processions visually symbolize our movement to the new Jerusalem. We are a people in pilgrimage. We are a pilgrim church, a church that walks with God toward God. We, like the Israelites of old, are a people on the move.

At times we as a choir may walk in formal processions. As wise choir directors and members know, doing so requires practice.

PRAYER

Most holy God,
remember your people
who cry beside the seductive rivers
of this world.
Help us not to forget you here on earth
so that, one day,
we may sing your songs
in the Jerusalem above.

"If we are not willing to listen to the sound of our own voice, why should anyone else bother to listen to it?" Katharine Le Mée, *Chant: The Origins, Form, Practice, and Healing Power of Gregorian Chant* (1994).

Jeremiah 31:31-34

Hebrews 5:7-9

Psalm 51:1-2, 10-11, 12-13

John 12:20-33

R. *Create a clean heart in me, O God.*

Have mercy on me, O God,
   according to your steadfast love;
according to your abundant mercy
   blot out my transgressions.
Wash me thoroughly from my iniquity,
   and cleanse me from my sin.

Create in me a clean heart, O God,
   and put a new and right spirit within me.
Do not cast me away from your presence,
   and do not take your holy spirit from me.

Restore to me the joy of your salvation,
   and sustain in me a willing spirit.
Then I will teach transgressors your ways,
   and sinners will return to you.

This, the fourth of the penitential psalms, is a prayer proclaiming repentance and requesting forgiveness.

Jeremiah pictures God as describing a "new" covenant, one based not upon eternal realities but upon what can be found in the human heart. One trait of this renewed covenant will be that God will forgive the people's "evil-doing and remember their sins no more." And so we can join the psalmist in praying: "Create a clean heart in me, O God, and put a new and right spirit within me."

FOR THE JOURNEY

In parts of England this Fifth Sunday of Lent was known as "Mothering Sunday." On this day people visited their mothers. It is likely that the custom was connected with the day's epistle reading which once was Galatians 4:21-31 wherein Paul speaks of the heavenly Jerusalem as the "mother of Christians."

28

Perhaps this medieval tradition can inspire us to remember our own mothers (and fathers) who passed on to many of us a love of music and singing. From them we have inherited a treasure that brings joy and delight to ourselves and to countless others. For those of us who are parents, there can be no greater gift than a love of music to hand on to our own children.

"O SACRED HEAD"

For many people Holy Week would not be complete without singing the *O Sacred Head Surrounded*.

The origin of its text is a long devotional poem, often—though erroneously—attributed to the French abbot Bernard of Clairvaux (1090-1153). The Latin poem has seven sections, each devoted to one part of Christ's physical body: feet, knees, hands, side, breast, heart, face (this last section entitled *Salve caput cruentatum*).

In the seventeenth century Paul Gerhardt (1607-1676), one of Germany's greatest hymn writers, translated the last section as *O Haupt voll Blut und Wunden*. In a very short time this German text was coupled with a melody written earlier by Hans Leo Hassler (1564-1612), an association that has happily lasted to the present.

Numerous translations have been made of Gerhardt's German text, perhaps the most common in Roman Catholic books being that of Henry Williams Baker (1821-1877), the compiler of a famous hymn collection, *Hymns Ancient and Modern* (1861).

PRAYER

Merciful and loving God,
your melodies constantly sing
of forgiveness and pardon.
Renew our hearts
with the joy and strength
of the Holy Spirit
so that we may celebrate your name
with newness of life
both here on earth
and one day in heaven.

"There is a singer's heart in the heart of God." Anon.

Passion Sunday (Palm Sunday)

Isaiah 50:4-7   Psalm 22:7-8, 16-17, 18-19, 22-23
Philippians 2:6-11   Mark 14:1-15:47 or 15:1-39

R. *My God, My God, why have you abandoned me?*

All who see me mock at me;
 they make mouths at me, they shake their heads;
"Commit your cause to the Lord; let him deliver—
 let him rescue the one in whom he delights!"

For dogs are all around me;
 a company of evildoers encircles me.
My hands and my feet have shriveled;
 I can count all my bones.

They divide my clothes among themselves,
 and for my clothing they cast lots.
But you, O Lord, do not be far away!
 O my help, come quickly to my aid!

Psalm 22, a messianic psalm which according to Catholic tradition especially refers to Christ, appears to have originally been three separate psalms: verses 2-22, a song of despair; verses 23-27, a call to praise; verses 28-32, a declaration that all people will worship God.

Many verses from this psalm can be found in the Passion accounts read during Holy Week. Verse 2, for example, "My God, my God . . ." (used as the antiphon) is placed upon the lips of Jesus on the cross.

FOR THE JOURNEY

Last year I spent Holy Week on Maryland's Eastern Shore, where on Thursday evening I participated in the Mass of the Lord's Supper in a small parish church.

The building itself could have used some liturgical face-lifting, but (as with all liturgical cele-bration) it was the people and the ministers who carried the day. The presider enjoyed what he was doing and, in his homily, showed that he understood what the evening's celebration and indeed all Holy Week were about. The deacon carried out his role

30

discreetly, unobtrusively. The reader understood the importance of phrase division in proclaiming the word. And the choir, perhaps ten or so members (together with organist/choir director) and located on one side up front, simply took visual and vocal delight in their ministry.

The assembly was small, perhaps numbering only seventy to eighty people. Yet the singing was robust and vigorous. It could only have been nurtured by a strong faith. The people obviously knew why they had gathered and were not afraid to express it in song. Something was very right in the church building that night. Worship was taking place.

PALM BRANCHES

Processing with palm branches on this day has its origins in fourth-century Jerusalem where the people, in imitation of Christ who was represented by the bishop, carried palms in procession on Palm Sunday afternoon.

When this practice spread to Europe (seventh and eighth centuries) the medieval flair for dramatic representation was let loose: Christ was represented by the blessed sacrament, by a gospel book on a carriage carried by the deacons, or by a carved figure seated on a wooden ass. The people carried palms or other greenery which, in years to come, would itself be blessed.

Although the procession with palms has long attracted the Christian imagination, the palm is not the focal point of today's celebration. It is Christ the victorious king, the innocent victim who is about "to save the guilty" (Preface) by his passion and death.

PRAYER

Most holy God,
your love for us is without measure;
it is always present.
Help our singing to be from the heart;
may it truly support
the prayer of those
who have gathered to praise you.

"If they won't sing it, they don't believe it." Anon.

Acts 10:34, 37-43　　　　　　　　　Psalm 118:1-2, 16-17, 22-23
Colossians 3:1-4 or 1 Corinthians 5:6-8　　　　　　　John 20:1-9

R. *This is the day the Lord has made;*
　let us rejoice and be glad. Or: *Alleluia.*

O give thanks to the Lord, for he is good;
　his steadfast love endures forever!
Let Israel say,
　"His steadfast love endures forever."

"The right hand of the Lord is exalted;
　the right hand of the Lord does valiantly."
I shall not die, but I shall live,
　and recount the deeds of the Lord.

The stone that the builders rejected
　has become the chief cornerstone.
This is the Lord's doing;
　it is marvelous in our eyes.

Perhaps speaking on behalf of the whole nation, the psalmist expresses gratitude for past and present deliverance.

Psalm 118 is the traditional Easter psalm in the Catholic Church. We, together with Christ, have been rescued from death; and so we will recount the deeds of the Lord. Verse 24 "This is the day . . ." appears as the antiphon.

FOR THE JOURNEY

To think of Easter as being merely the liturgical commemoration of Christ's resurrection is simply to miss the message. What is celebrated at Easter is not only Christ's historical coming forth from the dead but the power of Christ's resurrection upon our own lives. Our lives are resurrected lives. We join Christ in conquering death, and one day, because of Christ's victory, we too will rise from the dead.

Easter is about Christ and us "today." *This*, says the liturgy, is the day of salvation. Today is the day the Lord made. Christ is not the "I WAS" but the "I AM," still warming us with the fire of his love, still empowering us to be an Easter people, a people who can truly sing of an empty tomb, of puzzled disciples, and—just as importantly—of new life still shared today.

───────── WHY IS IT CALLED "EASTER"? ─────────

Pope Leo I (d.461) called it an "extraordinary day"; for Gregory Nazianzus (329-389) it was the "solemnity of solemnities" and the "queen of days"; for the early Christians its Latin name was *dies resurrectionis*; later on the Christian designation became *pascha* (from the Greek for "passover").

It is somewhat ironic that the origins of the English word for today's feast, the most solemn celebration of the liturgical year, are unclear. Venerable Bede (673-735), the "Father of English History," connected the word Easter to an Anglo-Saxon spring goddess named Eostre, and yet history gives no information as to the existence of such a personage. Perhaps Bede was just guessing here.

Many today theorize that the word derives from the Latin phrase for the week after the celebration of Christ's resurrection during which the newly baptized continued to wear their special baptismal garb, namely, the *hebdomada in albis* (the week of the white garments). The common folk misunderstood *in albis* as a plural of *alba*, namely dawn = *eostarum* in Old High German.

PRAYER

Eternal and all-powerful God,
with joy we give thanks to you for this day,
the day you have made.
May our voices,
inspired by the wonders of the Lord's resurrection,
sing of joy, victory, and life.

"Springtime is nature executing her Easter liturgy . . . In every corner of her vast cathedral a thousand voices are shouting Alleluia, the voices of creatures that have come to life. Yes, nature holy, sinless, eternal, is holding her Easter rites." Pius Parsch, *The Church's Year of Grace* (1954).

33

Acts 4:32-25   Psalm 118:2-4, 13-15, 22-24
1 John 5:1-6   John 20:19-31

R. *Give thanks to the Lord for he is good,*
    his love is everlasting.

Let Israel say,
  "His steadfast love endures forever."
Let the house of Aaron say,
  "His steadfast love endures forever."
Let those who fear the Lord say,
  "His steadfast love endures forever."

I was pushed hard, so that I was falling,
  but the Lord helped me.
The Lord is my strength and my might;
  he has become my salvation.
There are glad songs of victory
  in the tents of the righteous.

The stone that the builders rejected
  has become the chief cornerstone.
This is the Lord's doing;
  it is marvelous in our eyes.
This is the day the Lord has made;
  let us rejoice and be glad in it.

As on Easter, today's psalm is Psalm 118.

According to the Acts of the Apostles, "with power the apostles bore witness to the resurrection of the Lord Jesus . . ." Such witness to the resurrection is no less our calling since the faith, which we share with "one heart and one mind," has as its foundation the risen Lord Jesus. What the Father has done in Jesus Christ is "marvelous in our eyes," and for this reason we can "give thanks to the Lord."

FOR THE JOURNEY

Singing, some say, is the most   ancient and widespread form of music—no instrument is needed, just the human voice, and we can sing either by ourselves or with others.

Much of the time we halt all other activity while singing. For example, we sing *Happy Birthday*, and then we cut the cake. First *God Bless America*, and then the fireworks. The *Star Spangled Banner* is sung, and then the umpire yells "Play Ball!"

Yet not always. Sailors sing chanties while pulling ropes. People have sung while laying railroad tracks, while picking cotton, while working on the rock pile. On stage the members of the chorus sing while dancing. And then, of course, there is singing in the shower.

But have you ever come across any song designed to be sung while sinning? To sing is not to sin, since singing implies being in harmony with God, with self, and with others. Yes, we can even sing away the desire to sin.

HOLY WATER

The origins of blessing oneself with holy water upon entering a church are lost in antiquity, perhaps being connected with a somewhat widespread practice of washing before prayer. We know that fountains, at which the faithful washed their hands, were placed in the courtyards of many early Roman churches. When these courtyards were no longer constructed, this symbolic washing took place at the door of the church with the water placed in a vessel (called a stoup).

As we enter the church to join other members of Christ's Body for worship, we recall that we have been washed with the baptismal waters. We have been baptized in the name of the very Trinity whose sign we make. It is as a baptized people that we sing praise.

PRAYER

Most loving Father,
you have raised your Son
from the snares of death and destruction.
Help us to be strong in faith,
generous in love,
and joyful in song.

"These fifty days (of Pentecost) are celebrated after the Resurrection of the Lord as a figure not of work but of rest and joy. This is why we also cease to fast, and why we stand when we pray, which is the sign of the Resurrection." Augustine of Hippo (354-430).

Acts 3:13-15, 17-19   Psalm 4:1, 3, 6-7, 8
1 John 2:1-5   Luke 24:35-48

R. *Lord, let your face shine on us.*

Answer me when I call, O God of my right!
   You gave me room when I was in distress.
   Be gracious to me, and hear my prayer.

But know that the Lord has set apart the faithful for himself,
   the Lord hears when I call to him.

"Let the light of your face shine on us, O Lord!"
   You have put gladness in my heart.

I will both lie down and sleep in peace;
   for you alone, O Lord, make me lie down in safety.

Psalm 4, a song of trust and joyful confidence in God, has traditionally been used at night prayer (formerly known as Compline) in the
Roman Church.

Today's first reading concludes with Peter telling the people to
"reform your lives! Turn to God, that your sins may be wiped away!"
And the gospel selection concludes with Jesus saying that "penance for
the remission of sins is to be preached to all the nations . . ." A strange
theme for this Easter season of joy? But we can only come to joy once
we have heeded this call to repentance.

FOR THE JOURNEY

Jesus and Moses, as the story
goes, are playing a round of golf.
On coming to a rather short, par-
three hole, Jesus takes out his
seven iron. Moses, looking somewhat doubtful, suggests that a
short wood or at least a five iron
might be better. But Jesus responds: "If Arnold Palmer can do

it, so can I."

With that, Jesus hits the ball
directly into a water hazard half-
way down the fairway. Moses
offers to get the ball. Going to
the water, he "does his thing";
raising his arms in a dramatic
gesture, he parts the water and
then retrieves the ball.

Jesus again tees-off—and with the same club. Again Moses remonstrates, but Jesus says: "If Arnold Palmer can do it, so can I." And he drops his ball into the exact spot in the water. This time Jesus says he will get it himself, so he goes to the water and "does his act," calmly walking across the pond and then reaching in.

Just at this moment the next foursome comes up. One man, looking at Jesus walking on the water, says to Moses: "Now just who does that fellow think he is, Jesus Christ?" Moses replies: "No, unfortunately, Arnold Palmer."

What we believe about ourselves (either individually or as a group) can have a tremendous impact on what we think we can accomplish and even on what we actually do accomplish.

RELIGIOUS/CHURCH/SACRED MUSIC

Church choirs do not ordinarily sing choral arrangements of Broadway show tunes. But what do we call the music that we sing?

Within recent years various terms have emerged, and people often use them interchangeably.

Religious Music, a somewhat vague yet all-embracing term, designates music having a religious theme, anything from a Gregorian selection to a Hindu chant, from Bach's *Passion* to Bernstein's *Mass*.

Church Music, which in popular speech is often equated with religious music, specifies the place where the music is performed, in the church.

Sacred Music, although commonly used for religious music, is the term found in many church documents as specifying the music used for the liturgy, with the word "sacred" being opposed to "profane" music.

PRAYER

Eternal God,
you have done wonders
by delivering us, through Christ,
from the sorrow of sin and death.
Open our hearts.
Let us find your peace and joy
as we sing our Easter songs of praise.

"The primary form of Christian music is singing." Universa Laus, *Beliefs Held in Common*, no. 16.

Acts 4:8-12   Psalm 118:1, 8-9, 21-23, 36, 21, 29
1 John 3:1-12   John 10:11-18

R. *The stone rejected by the builders*
   has become the cornerstone.

O give thanks to the Lord, for he is good;
   his steadfast love endures forever!
It is better to take refuge in the Lord
   than to put confidence in mortals.
It is better to take refuge in the Lord
   than to put confidence in princes.

I thank you that you have answered me
   and have become my salvation.
The stone that the builders rejected
   has become the chief cornerstone.
This is the Lord's doing;
   it is marvelous in our eyes.

Blessed is the one who comes in the name of the Lord.
   We bless you from the house of the Lord.
I thank you that you have answered me
   and have become my salvation.
O give thanks to the Lord, for he is good,
   for his steadfast love endures forever.

Today's responsorial is again Psalm 118, used on Easter Sunday and on the Second Sunday of Easter.

In the first reading Peter is questioned: in whose name has he cured the man who was crippled. The apostle responds that he has done so in the name of Jesus who is "the stone rejected by you the builders which has become the cornerstone," a quotation from Psalm 118, today's responsorial psalm.

FOR THE JOURNEY

Music, unlike many other forms   of art, never looks back. Indeed, for it to be music, the piece must always go onward, must proceed ahead. We can always flip back a few pages in a novel, back-up the film, return our eyes to the very same painting time and time again. But the melody, once begun, simply moves on, pulling us with it. And so, as singers, we are told to "sing to the end of the phrase," "to push forward and intensify" a held note, to prepare for a page turn lest we be left behind.

In a way music is a symbol of the Christian life. It is always a journey, always a pilgrimage with Christ as the guide. We can never turn back. True, year after year we do return to the same Lenten and Easter songs and sing them as we did before. And yet not really, for we are always progressing toward that Jerusalem where past, present, and future come together, eternally suspended in a familiar yet ever new psalm of praise.

LITURGICAL/PASTORAL MUSIC

To continue with the various terms used to describe the music we sing in our worship . . .

Liturgical Music—the designation became popular only in the 1960s —looks to the functional link between music and worship. It stresses that the music is wedded to the liturgy, either the music being part of the liturgical action (e.g., the singing of the *Holy, Holy*) or as accompanying an action of the liturgy (the singing of a psalm during the communion procession).

Another term, used in the U.S., is *Pastoral Music,* referring to music suitable for use on the parish level, including liturgy, religious education, social justice programs, etc.

> **PRAYER**
> Merciful and loving God,
> you have given us
> a new and spiritual creation
> in the person of your Son, Jesus Christ.
> Help us to bless and praise you
> with hearts full of joy,
> wonder, and love.

"See that your praise comes from you whole being; in other words, see that you praise God not with your lips and voices alone, but with your minds, your lives, and all your actions." Augustine of Hippo (354-430).

Acts 9:26-31   Psalm 22:25-26, 27, 29, 30-31
1 John 3:18-24   John 15:1-8

R. *I will praise you, Lord, in the assembly of your people.*

My vows I will pay before those who fear him.
The poor shall eat and be satisfied;
   those who seek him shall praise the Lord.
   May your hearts live forever!

All the ends of the earth shall remember
   and turn to the Lord;
and all the families of the nations
   shall worship before him.
For dominion belongs to the Lord,
   and he rules over the nations.
To him, indeed, shall all who sleep in the earth bow down;
   before him shall bow all who go down to the dust.

And I shall live for him.
Posterity will serve him;
   future generations will be told about the Lord,
and proclaim his deliverance to a people yet unborn,
   saying that he has done it.

Psalm 22 was used as the responsorial psalm on Passion Sunday.

Today we hear Christ saying that he is the vine and that we, as his disciples, are to bear much fruit. To state it differently, we are to "build up the body of Christ." The early church was very aware of this mission; the "church was at peace . . . was being built up and was making steady progress in the fear of the Lord." We are not only to praise the Lord in the assembly of the people, but are also to work for the day when "all the families of the nations shall worship" the Lord.

FOR THE JOURNEY

"Nothing great was ever achieved without enthusiasm" wrote Ralph Waldo Emerson (1803-1882). Enthusiasm means having strong feelings, zeal, joyous energy, excitement. It is the ability to see the glory, to rejoice, to be glad in the work at hand.

Enthusiastic athletes win medals; enthusiastic teachers motivate students; enthusiastic fans help the home team win

Enthusiastic choir members are a joy to sing with, a joy to direct, a joy to listen to, and a joy to know, for they are a sign of what awaits us all. As St. Theophane Venard phrased it: "Be merry, really merry. The life of a true Christian should be a perpetual jubilee, a prelude to the festivals of eternity."

MASS IN THE CATACOMBS?

The picture of the early Christians hiding from the Romans soldiers and celebrating Mass each week in the Roman catacombs has been—and perhaps remains—quite popular. Yet it is simply not true; it is a myth popularized by Cardinal Nicholas Wiseman's widely read novel *Fabiola, or the Church of the Catacombs,* published in London (1854).

The earliest Christian communities, we must remember, were relatively small, and so it was quite easy for its members to worship in private homes, especially in the dwellings of the more affluent members. The catacombs, on the other hand, were underground cemeteries where the faithful (and others) buried their dead.

It was only after the persecutions ended in the fourth century that Christian worship became more public, and large civic meeting halls (basilicas) were used. This change greatly affected the liturgy itself, which grew to "fit" the building: thus the appearance of processions, musical expansion, the development of ceremonial, etc.

PRAYER
Most holy God,
through Jesus Christ
death has been conquered
and life has been renewed.
May we always recognize
the saving power of Christ among us.
May our Alleluias always express
our enduring love for you.

"This church has been built for you, but it is rather you who are the church."
Augustine of Hippo (354-430).

41

Acts 10:25-26, 34-35, 44-48   Psalm 98:1, 2-3, 3-4
1 John 4:7-10   John 15:9-17

R. *The Lord has revealed to the nations his saving power.*

O sing to the Lord a new song,
  for he has done marvelous things.
His right hand and his holy arm
  have gotten him victory.

The Lord has made known his victory;
  he has revealed his vindication
  in the sight of the nations.
He has remembered his steadfast love and faithfulness
  to the house of Israel.

All the ends of the earth have seen
  the victory of our God.
Make a joyful noise to the Lord, all the earth;
  break forth into joyous song and sing praises.

Psalm 98 was also used as the responsorial psalm on Christmas Day.
The general motif of today's readings is God's love. Jesus tells us: "As the Father has loved me, so I have loved you . . ." And John says that "God is love . . . (and) love consists in this: not that we have loved God, but that God has loved us . . ." In the Acts of the Apostles we find that the early Jewish Christians "were surprised that the gift of the Holy Spirit should have been poured out on the Gentiles also." God's saving love has no bounds—it extends to peoples everywhere: "The Lord has revealed to the nations his saving power."

FOR THE JOURNEY

There are still quite a few Catholics who at times remark: "I wish the church would do something about it." By "church" they mean the pope, the various Roman ecclesiastical offices, the bishop, the parish priest. The church exists "out there."

But just what is the church? Theologians have long searched

42

for an answer. To be sure, the church is hard to define; perhaps it is more easily described. Down through the ages many theological images have been used to convey various aspects of the church, but the bottom line always remains: "The church is *us*."

We, in all our human genius and messiness, with warts and beauty marks, form the church. And when we come together to hear God's word and celebrate the eucharist, when we listen and respond, when we speak and sing, we make the church visible in a particular place. We experience what we *are*, members of one Body, sharing one faith, united in common song.

HOMILY OR SERMON?

The word "homily," from the Greek for "instruction" or "conversation," was used as early as the third century to describe the explanation of the scriptures during the liturgy of the word.

During the Middle Ages, however, preachers often departed from the traditional form and gave devotional or moralistic exhortations divorced from the biblical texts. In many ways such preaching (called the "sermon") was not even considered as being integral to the Mass itself.

The present century, especially with Vatican II, has seen a return to the church's ancient practice: the preacher is to preach on the scriptural word that has been proclaimed; preaching is considered not as an adjunct to but as an essential part of the liturgy of the word.

In Roman Catholic terminology especially, this biblical preaching is called the "homily," whereas the word "sermon" is often used to describe a more general religious exhortation.

PRAYER

Eternal God,
you have renewed all things
through the resurrection of your Son.
May our song at the eucharist
be a sign of love and respect
for all creation,
for all you have entrusted to our care.

"After eating it is expected that everyone sing God's praises, however he is able, whether from the holy Scriptures or out of his own talent." Tertullian (c.160-c.220).

43

Acts 1:15-17, 20-26
1 John 4:11-16

Psalm 103:1-2, 11-12, 19-20
John 17:11-19

R. *The Lord has set his throne in heaven.*

Bless the Lord, O my soul,
  and all that is within me,
  bless his holy name.
Bless the Lord, O my soul,
  and do not forget all his benefits.

For as the heavens are high above the earth,
  so great is his steadfast love
  toward those who fear him;
as far as the east is from the west,
  so far he removes our transgressions from us.

The Lord has established his throne in the heavens,
  and his kingdom rules over all.
Bless the Lord, O you his angels,
  you mighty ones who do his bidding.

Our God is good and merciful; our God is a saving and healing God. For this reason the psalmist in Psalm 103 praises the divine goodness.

God's love and care are the predominant themes in today's second and third readings. Jesus, praying to his Father, requests that the disciples be protected "with your name which you have given me." And the conclusion of our second reading is the famous "God is love and whoever abides in love abides in God and God in him." We indeed are to "bless the Lord"—"so great is his steadfast love toward those who fear him."

FOR THE JOURNEY

This Easter Season has been a time to sing about and celebrate many things, but our attention has primarily been focused upon life: Christ's new and resurrected life, our participation in this life by means of baptism, the grace-filled lives of the recently baptized. Even nature seems to reflect this fascination with life and with its reawakening around us: the trees, the grass, the bushes, the spring flowers.

Yet unlike nature, we have to choose life, doing so deliberately and consciously day after day. This is what it means to be a Christian. And we do so with the help of the Holy Spirit, the life-giving breath of God, the Spirit whom we have already received and for whose coming we continue to pray—another wonderful paradox of our faith.

——————— "SING A LITTLE, DANCE A LITTLE . . . " ———————

Most of us have sung melodies identified as being "Shaker" tunes, e.g., Sydney Carter's *I Danced in the Morning*, but perhaps many have little idea of who the Shakers were.

The group, which originated in a 1747 Quaker revival in England, settled in the woods of Watervliet near Albany, NY. At one time there were about five to six thousand members in the U.S., in eighteen settlements, but today, for all purposes, the group is extinct.

The Shakers held all property in common, arose at a common hour, took meals together, abstained from smoking, were pacifists, and—although marriage was not absolutely forbidden—placed the highest value on celibacy (obviously one reason for the drastic decline in their numbers).

The members of the group were known to "shake" with spiritual excitement during their religious services at which dancing played a prominent part. One Shaker prescription for worship was: "Sing a little, dance a little, exhort a little, preach a little, and a good many littles will make a great deal."

> ### PRAYER
> Compassionate and loving God,
> through the waters of baptism
> you forgive our sins and renew our youth.
> Help us to serve you
> with joyful voices
> and with loving hearts.

"For me to believe in their Redeemer, Christians would have to sing better songs, and they would have to look more redeemed." Friedrich Wilhelm Nietzsche (1844-1900).

Acts 2:1-11
1 Corinthians 12:3-7, 12-13

Psalm 104:1, 24, 29-30, 31, 34
John 20:19-23

R. *Lord, send out your Spirit,*
   and renew the face of the earth.

Bless the Lord, O my soul,
   O Lord my God, you are very great.
O Lord, how manifold are your works!
   The earth is full of your creatures.

When you take away their breath, they die
   and return to their dust.
When you send forth your spirit, they are created;
   and you renew the face of the earth.

May the glory of the Lord endure forever;
   may the Lord rejoice in his works!
May my meditation be pleasing to him,
   for I rejoice in the Lord.

Here the psalmist, exhibiting gratitude to God, praises the divine wisdom and extols certain wonderful features of creation.

Today's readings focus on the Holy Spirit who will "renew the face of the earth." As Christians we have indeed been renewed and transformed through the Spirit-filled waters of baptism. We have been anointed with the power of the life-giving Spirit. We are also called to "renew the face of the earth." God's work is our work.

FOR THE JOURNEY

Liturgy has very often been compared to the world of "make-believe." When we gather to worship we enter a world where we often pretend, as it were, that peace, love, and justice already exist on earth. We request sal-vation and yet the Savior of the world has already come. We dare to share the sign of peace with one another even though true peace may be lacking. We have been anointed with the Holy Spirit at baptism and yet, as if unaware of this, our prayers request the Spirit's coming. There is indeed much wonderful fantasy in our Christian world.

The world of song is also a "make-believe" world, one where life's unpleasantries give way to the flow of melody, to the rush of rhythm, to the wonders of mysteriously changing harmonies. Through music we can leave our present space and enter a new, constantly challenging universe with its own time, its own colors, its own landscape.

Song has the power to transport us to lands we merely dream of, to kingdoms we cannot imagine, to cities we never knew existed. Music, not all that different from worship itself, is a fantasy world, one in which we can truly make merry, sing, play, and dance with God.

"COME HOLY GHOST "

There was a time when no Confirmation or Pentecost would be complete without the singing of this hymn.

The Latin text upon which it is based, *Veni, Creator Spiritus*, most probably originated in the ninth century, and it has been attributed to the German theologian Rabanus Maurus (776 or 784-856). As early as the tenth century it was assigned as a Vespers hymn for Pentecost.

Down through the centuries numerous English translations of the hymn have been made, the most commonly used being that of Edward Caswall (1814-1878).

The familiar melody was composed by the French Jesuit Louis Lambillotte (1796-1855); it was first published with a Marian text in his *Chants à Marie* (1843). Later in life Lambillotte became a leader in the restoration of chant and attempted to distance himself from his early musical work.

PRAYER
O God of life and of light,
you have created visible things to lead us
to what the eye cannot see.
Send your Spirit upon us so that
under a new heaven and on a new earth
we may sing the glory of your name.

"An unsung liturgy, no matter how frequent its doing, is an abnormal liturgy." Aidan Kavanagh, O.S.B. In *Music in Catholic Worship: The NPM Commentary* (1982).

47

Deuteronomy 4:32-34, 39-40   Psalm 33:4-5, 6, 9, 18-19, 20, 22
Romans 8:14-17   Matthew 28:16-20

R. *Happy the people the Lord has chosen to be his own.*

For the word of the Lord is upright,
    and all his work is done in faithfulness.
He loves righteousness and justice;
    the earth is full of the steadfast love of the Lord.

By the word of the Lord the heavens were made,
    and all their host by the breath of his mouth.
For he spoke and it came to be;
    he commanded, and it stood firm.

Truly the eye of the Lord is on those who fear him,
    on those who hope in his steadfast love,
to deliver their soul from death,
    and to keep them alive in famine.

Our soul waits for the Lord;
    he is our help and hour shield.
Let your steadfast love, O Lord, be upon us,
    even as we hope in you.

Psalm 33 praises the Lord's power and fidelity.

The first reading is from the Book of Deuteronomy where Moses is making a case for the God who acts on behalf of the Jewish people because of divine love. "Did a people ever hear the voice of God speaking from the midst of the fire . . .?" Continuing this theme, the responsorial psalm recalls that "the word of the Lord is upright, and all his work is done in faithfulness."

FOR THE JOURNEY

One of the things about rituals is that they are repeated over and over again. You just can't sit down and *create* a ritual (a ceremony, yes, but not a ritual). This element of repeatability provides the rite's participants with a certain degree of stability and familiarity—everyone knows what's coming next. There is a high comfort level, like wearing a favorite pair of shoes, or joining in a dance whose steps come naturally, or singing a song familiar since childhood.

When we sing familiar pieces known so well by choir and people alike, we add another thread to that rich texture of action, posture, silence, and speech we call liturgy. These songs link us to a past we cannot escape.

Yet the old is to be balanced by the new since each of us is constantly becoming a new person in Christ, since today the fullness of God's kingdom is closer than it was yesterday.

TRINITY SUNDAY

Most Christian feasts have their basis in historical events, e.g., Christ's birth, Christ's resurrection. But there are a few feasts, usually introduced into the liturgical calendar more recently, that recall a point of doctrine (e.g., Trinity Sunday) or are designed to teach a lesson (e.g., Feast of the Holy Family). These are known as "idea" or "didactic" feasts.

Although special liturgical prayers in honor of the Trinity can be found as early as the eighth century, the popes long rejected the idea of having a special Trinitarian feast in the liturgical calendar. It was only in 1334 that this celebration was authorized for the universal church.

Today's liturgy is not the place to attempt theological explanations into the deep mystery of God, but it is the place to praise and celebrate the goodness and love of God who shares divine life with us through Jesus Christ and through the Holy Spirit.

PRAYER

Lord God,
our protection and our guide,
you have chosen us to be your people.
Make us a sign of your own unity.
Make our song reflect a oneness of heart,
of faith, and of spirit.

"See that what you sing with your mouth, you believe in your heart. What you believe in your heart prove by your deeds." A medieval formula used for the blessing of singers.

Exodus 24:3-8
Hebrews 9:11-15

Psalm 116:12-13, 15-16, 17-18
Mark 14:12-16, 22-26

R. *I will take the cup of salvation,*
and call on the name of the Lord.

What shall I return to the Lord
for all his bounty to me?
I will lift up the cup of salvation
and call on the name of the Lord.

Precious in the sight of the Lord
is the death of his faithful ones.
O Lord, I am your servant;
I am your servant, the child of your serving girl.
You have loosed my bonds.

I will offer to you a thanksgiving sacrifice
and call on the name of the Lord.
I will pay my vows to the Lord
in the presence of all his people.

Psalm 116 was used on the Second Sunday of Lent.

Today's gospel highlights the eucharist as being the sacrifice of the "new covenant." This new relationship between God and humankind is founded in Christ and is closely related to the accomplishment of the fullness of the kingdom. The Old Testament reading has Moses speaking about the blood of the covenant sprinkled upon the people. But in the new dispensation it is no longer the blood of animals that cleanses. For our part, we long to share in this offering: "I will lift up the cup of salvation . . ."

FOR THE JOURNEY

There is an ancient church document whose English title is *The Catholic Teaching of the Twelve Apostles.* Written in Syria during the third century, the work treats a variety of topics: the duties of the bishop, the role of the deacon, the pardon of sinners, fasting, etc.

Here is what it says about the members of the assembly and its meetings: "Let them not fail to attend, but let them gather faithfully together. Let no one deprive the church by staying away; if they do, they deprive the body of Christ of one of its members."

What a powerful thought! If they are absent, "they deprive the Body of Christ of one of its members." What is true for the assembly is no less true for the choir.

___ SOLEMNITY OF THE BODY AND BLOOD OF CHRIST ___

Today's feast honors in a special way Christ's presence in the eucharist.

Certainly as Scripture and the church's tradition demonstrate, the purpose of the eucharist is to be our food: "Take and eat . . . Take and drink." Although this "taking" usually occurred within the celebration of the Lord's Supper, the early church did reserve the eucharist for those who were unable to be present for the celebration, e.g., the sick, the imprisoned, and eventually those about to die.

In time—and for a variety of reasons—the number of people receiving communion dramatically decreased. As a result, devotion to the reserved sacrament greatly increased, with prayers before the eucharist, visits to the blessed sacrament, and reservation of the sacrament on or near the altar. Out of such a religious climate today's feast was born in the thirteenth century.

Although frequent communion has today been restored, the church's love for the reserved eucharist remains one of its most cherished traditions. Our devotion to the blessed sacrament is to flow from, and lead us back to, that sacred meal given us by Christ himself.

PRAYER

Lord Jesus Christ,
you gave us the eucharist
to be our spiritual food and drink.
Allow us to taste and sing on earth
the glories of the meal
you have prepared for us in heaven.

"The soul of one who loves God always swims in joy, always keeps holiday, and is always in the mood for singing." John of the Cross (1542-1591).

1 Samuel 3:3-10, 19   Psalm 40:1, 3, 6-7, 7-8, 9
1 Corinthians 6:13-15, 17-20   John 1:35-42

R. *Here am I, Lord;*
  I come to do your will.

I waited paitently for the Lord;
  he inclined to me and heard my cry.
He put a new song in my mouth,
  a song of praise to our God.

Sacrifice and offering you do not desire,
  but you have given me an open ear.
Burnt offering and sin offering you have not required.
Then I said, "Here I am."

"In the scroll of the book it is written of me.
I delight to do your will, O my God;
  your law is within my heart.

I have told the glad news of deliverance
  in the great congregation;
see, I have not restrained my lips,
  as you know, O Lord.

Psalm 40 has two sections (vv. 1-11 and vv. 12-17), each of which probably was a distinct composition. Praise is the dominant theme in the first part, whereas supplication predominates in part two.

God's call permeates today's liturgy of the word. In the gospel we hear the Lord calling the two disciples. And it is the call of Samuel which is presented in the first reading. We are always being called by God. To do God's will is "our delight."

FOR THE JOURNEY

"In 1983, a student at Colorado State University charged a Fort Collins priest with throwing her down a flight of stairs for playing the tambourine poorly during Mass. According to the student, the priest told her, 'You play the same way over and over again.

You're not going to play at 5:15 Mass anymore'—and then threw her out the door and down the stairs." (From John Dollison, *Pope-Pourri*, New York: Simon & Schuster, 1984.)

The clergy in Colorado (or at least some of them) take very seriously the music played during the liturgy. And yet, we are told, choirs that practice very diligently are usually safe from such outbursts of clerical disapproval, both in Colorado and elsewhere.

THE PSALMS—RELIGIOUS POETRY

Throughout its history the church has known a wide variety of prayers, but none does it hold more precious than the psalms. No Mass is celebrated, no sacrament is celebrated, no liturgy of the hours is prayed, without the psalms. They are used in both east and west by Christians of all denominations. They are prayed by our Jewish brothers and sisters throughout the world.

The Bible contains much religious poetry (e.g., Genesis 4:23f, Numbers 21:17f, Isaiah 23:16f, etc.). In addition to the psalter, the Old Testament contains other complete books (e.g., the Song of Songs) written in poetry. But the Book of Psalms has always been a special jewel in Israel's tradition of religious poetry.

Although we know few details, many of the psalms were connected with the temple service in Jerusalem where they were accompanied by a wide variety of instruments. This association of musical instruments was so strong that when the Hebrew text of the psalms was rendered into Greek, the Greek word *psalmos* (literally the "twanging of a harp") was used to designate these poems.

Other psalms are of a more private nature, the prayer of an individual speaking alone to God.

PRAYER

Lord God,
you have given us the gift of creation,
a mirror of your own goodness and wonder.
May our eyes ever feast in your beauty,
our ears always hear your voice,
and our lips always sing your song.

"It is the assembly and not the place that I call 'church'." Clement of Alexandria (c.150-c.215).

Jonah 3:1-5, 10
1 Corinthians 7:29-31

Psalm 25:4-5, 6-7, 8-9
Mark 1:14-20

R. *Teach me your ways, O Lord.*

Make me to know your ways, O Lord;
  teach me your paths.
Lead me in your truth, and teach me,
  for you are the God of my salvation.

Be mindful of your mercy, O Lord,
  and of your steadfast Love,
  for they have been from of old.
According to your steadfast love remember me,
  for your goodness' sake, O Lord.

Good and upright is the Lord;
  therefore he instructs sinners in the way.
He leads the humble in what is right,
  and teaches the humble in his way.

Psalm 25 was used earlier this year on the First Sunday of Lent.

Today's gospel speaks about repentance and about responding to God's invitation (Jesus calling the first disciples). The same two motifs occur in the first reading with Jonah who obeys God's command and goes to preach conversion to the pagan Ninevites. We too are to listen and respond to God: we pray that God's ways be made known to us: "Teach me your ways, O Lord."

FOR THE JOURNEY

The years immediately following the Second Vatican Council were marked with great excitement and activity in regard to ecumenism and the eventual removal of the painful divisions existing within Christianity. Today, however, the pace of interfaith dialogue has perhaps slowed, with some crucial issues (e.g., the ordination of women) appearing to be insoluble. And yet progress continues.

Study into the origins of Christian liturgy has resulted in a remarkable similarity of worship structures (liturgy of word and liturgy of table) among many denominations; in many churches the same scriptural readings as found in our Roman Lectionary are proclaimed each Sunday. And texts from the German Protestant tradition (e.g., Martin Luther's *A Mighty Fortress*) and the English Protestant tradition (e.g., Charles Wesley's *Love Divine, All Loves Excelling* or Isaac Watts' *O God, Our Help in Ages Past*) are sung by Roman Catholics, whereas a number of Protestant hymnals and service books have incorporated some English translations of medieval Latin hymns used in the Roman liturgy.

In spite of all, the Holy Spirit—the Spirit of unity—continues to work among us.

KING DAVID?

According to early Jewish and Christian thinking, David was the author of the majority, if not all, of the psalms.

But did David actually sit down, so to speak, and compose the psalms? Although scholarship would not necessarily exclude David as the author of at least some of these poems, it appears that the psalter was composed over a period of many centuries, and it includes material pre-dating the monarchy (before the eleventh century) and extending down to the sixth century B.C.

Some of the psalms were first grouped together as small "collections." These were then formed into "books" and then into the psalter as it has come down to us. A process of editing and revision occurred before and during this period.

> **PRAYER**
> Father, Lord of all creation,
> many of your deeds are on our behalf.
> Help us to find your presence
> in all that we do.
> May we hear a little bit of heaven
> in every song we sing.

"The psalms profit us most when they give God most Glory. This they do when we realize that the Liturgy is not a search for something we have not, but the celebration of what we already have." Thomas Merton, *Bread in the Wilderness* (1960).

Deuteronomy 18:15-20

Psalm 95:1-2, 6-7, 7-9

1 Corinthians 7:32-25

Mark 1:21-28

R. *If today you hear his voice,
harden not your hearts.*

O come, let us sing to the Lord;
let us make a joyful noise to the rock of our salvation!
Let us come into his presence with thanksgiving;
let us make a joyful noise to him with songs of praise.

O come, let us worship and bow down,
let us kneel before the Lord, our Maker!
For he is our God,
and we are the people of his pasture,
and the sheep of his hand.

O that today you would listen to his voice!
Do not harden your hearts, as at Meribah,
as on the day at Massah in the wilderness,
when your ancestors tested me,
and put me to the proof,
though they had seen my work.

Psalm 95 invites us to praise and worship the Lord.

God often speaks to us through other human beings. Today's first reading relates how Moses was chosen to speak in place of God; Moses thus was the first in a long line of prophets. We, like the people of old, are called to hear God's voice with open, not closed hearts.

FOR THE JOURNEY

The Washington, DC area is noted for its many and technically proficient choral groups. Among the most famous of these is the Paul Hill Chorale, an organization of some 180 voices. Its director is now confined to a wheelchair and is soon to retire.

A recent newspaper article reported the selection of a successor to Mr. Hill, who explained to the reporter that the Chorale was by design an all-purpose choral group, capable of performing compositions by both traditional and contemporary composers. The reporter went on to question the conductor as to the secret of the Chorale's success. Hill's reply: "Work, work, work."

Not all that bad a recipe for every choral group! And for every choir director!

BOOKS WITHIN A BOOK

As mentioned last week, the biblical psalter is actually made up of five smaller "books": I = Psalms 1-41; II = Psalms 42-72; III = Psalms 73-89; IV = Psalms 90-106; V = Psalms 107-150. This is one of the psalter's unique features.

A distinguishing mark of these smaller books is the manner in which they address God. For example, Books I, IV, and V usually address God as Yahweh (Lord); Book II usually employs Elohim (God); whereas Book III uses both types of address. Another feature is that the concluding psalm in each book ends with a doxology.

The Church Fathers as well as Jewish tradition linked this five-fold division with the five books of the Pentateuch. And yet collecting the psalms into separate books was probably not the work of a single editor since there is a duplication of psalms, e.g., two psalms in Book I are repeated in Book II: Psalm 14 = 53 and Psalm 40:13-17 = 70.

PRAYER
Eternal and loving God,
you have given us Jesus
as our saving rock.
Give strength to our spirits,
make merry our hearts,
and fill us with love
so that our song be
ever worthy of your name.

"When God saw that many men were lazy, and gave themselves only with difficulty to spiritual reading, he wished to make it easy for them, and added the melody to the prophet's words, that all being rejoiced by the charm of the music, should sing hymns to him with gladness." John Chrysostom (347-407) explaining why the psalms are sung.

Job 7:1-4, 6-7   Psalm 147:1-2, 3-4, 5-6
1 Corinthians 9:16-19, 22-23   Mark 1:29-39

R. *Praise the Lord, who heals the brokenhearted.*

Praise the Lord!
How good it is to sing praises to our God;
  for he is gracious, and a song of praise is fitting.
The Lord builds up Jerusalem;
  he gathers the outcasts of Israel.

He heals the brokenhearted,
  and binds up their wounds.
He determines the number of the stars;
  he gives to all of them their names.

Great is our Lord, and abundant in power;
  his understanding is beyond measure.
The Lord lifts up the downtrodden;
  he casts the wicked to the ground.

Psalm 147 can be divided into three parts (vv. 1-6, vv.7-11, and vv. 12-20). In this section the God who has created the stars is pictured as the God who also saves the weak and who rescues the outcasts.

Human pain and suffering have long been an enigma to the religious person. Job is angry, frustrated, and even bitter: "My days . . . come to an end without hope." How often Job's plight seems to be our own. We can do nothing other than join the psalmist in a song of trust: God "heals the brokenhearted and binds up their wounds."

FOR THE JOURNEY

A common assumption today is that worship is to be beautiful, whether it be a small group liturgy celebrated with classic simplicity or a Mass in St. Peter's Basilica carried out with the utmost of solemnity and majesty. People just want to pray with the help of what they consider beautiful buildings, art, texts, and music.

At any rate, the liturgy stands in stark contrast with what is found in so many corners of our lives and our world: radio and TV commercials, the assault of billboards on our eyes, the gridlock paralyzing our major expressways.

And so we take delight in another world. We are transported to a land where we may experience, if only partially and briefly, the beauty of a God who surpasses our wildest imaginations and whose music constantly awaits our voices.

WHY DIFFERENT NUMBERS?

Have you ever noticed that the numbering of the psalms sometimes differs from one source to another? For example, the psalm "The Lord is my shepherd" at times appears as Psalm 22 and at other times as Psalm 23. The reason is found within the history of the biblical text.

It was from about 250 B.C. to the first century B.C. that the Hebrew Scriptures were translated into Greek for the benefit of Jews living in Alexandria. There exists a letter, no doubt relating fiction, stating that seventy-two scholars were summoned from Jerusalem to the isle of Pharos where in seventy-two days they completed a Greek version of the Pentateuch (the first five books of the Bible). Thus the term Septuagint (seventy = LXX) came to be applied to the Greek translation of the Hebrew books as a whole, even though the task of translating actually spanned a very long period of time.

As to the Book of Psalms, twice the Greek translation combines what are separate psalms in the Hebrew, and twice it makes two separate psalms out of what is a single psalm in the Hebrew. As a result, the Septuagint is one number behind the Hebrew for much of the psalter (the numbering of the first eight psalms and the last three psalms is identical in both versions). In the past the Septuagint numbering was followed in the church's liturgical use of the psalms. Today, however, the Roman lectionary uses the Hebrew numbering.

> **PRAYER**
> Father of all holiness,
> you are the author
> of all good things.
> Help us to celebrate in song
> our love for you
> and for all you have created.

"He was a singer of the songs of David." Inscription on a fifth-century tomb.

Leviticus 13:1-2, 44-46

1 Corinthians 10:31-11:1

Psalm 32:1-2, 5, 11

Mark 1:40-45

R. *I turn to you, Lord, in time of trouble,*
and you fill me with the joy of salvation.

Happy are those whose transgression is forgiven,
    whose sin is covered.
Happy are those to whom the Lord imputes no iniquity,
    and in whose spirit there is no deceit.

Then I acknowledged my sin to you,
    and I did not hide my iniquity.
I said, "I will confess my transgressions to the Lord,"
    and you forgave the guilt of my sin.

Be glad in the Lord and rejoice, O righteous,
    and shout for joy, all you upright of heart.

Psalm 32, the second of the "penitential psalms," praises the Lord whose forgiving grace is all-powerful.

Sin and sickness constantly appear on the pages of both Old and New Testaments. Today's gospel presents us with Jesus curing the leper; the first reading contains the prescription that the leper be "expelled" from the community. Physical sickness calls for healing; no less is true for spiritual sickness which we refer to as sin. With the psalmist we too can "turn to the Lord in time of trouble." Doing so we obtain forgiveness which in turn results in a joyful spirit, allowing us to "shout for joy."

FOR THE JOURNEY

After almost twenty centuries of Christianity much evil still exists in the world. The morning newspaper and the evening news on TV are daily witnesses of this with their accounts of bombings, murders, spousal a-buse, deadly accidents caused by drunk and speeding drivers, etc.

Even the church and the local parish can suffer the ravaging effects of unconverted hearts:

mistrust, jealousy, division, name-calling, petty rivalries, accusations of various sorts. All weaken the Body of Christ.

Nonetheless, we continue to sing. Why so? Not to avoid acknowledging the wounds affecting society and our faith community. We sing to proclaim that evil will not endure, that greed will give way to generosity, that strife will be transformed into peace. There is an old gospel song (its title is *Face to Face*) that goes: "What rejoicing in his presence, when are banished grief and pain, when the crooked ways are straightened and the dark things shall be plain."

_____ CRYPTIC JOTTINGS _____

When you pray the psalms from the Bible itself, you have no doubt noticed that many of these poems have short cryptic words at their beginning, e.g., "To the leader; on Lilies, a Covenant. Of A'Saph. A Psalm" (Ps 80).

The inscriptions, added by editors down through the ages, are not part of the inspired text and their meaning at times still puzzle biblical scholars. Many of these jotting, however, refer to the performance of the psalms, whether it be musical forms or assigned melodies or instrumental accompaniments.

Although no ancient Hebrew melody or instrument has come down to us, a vast array of musical resources appear to have been brought to the psalms, especially when they were sung in temple worship.

PRAYER

Merciful Father,
you forgive the sinner
and support the weak.
Help us to overcome evil
and to let go of fear.
Make us strong in faith,
constant in prayer,
and joyful in song.

"The psalms are "the blessing of the people, the glory of God, the praise of the people, the applause of all, the language of the assembly, the voice of the church, the sweet sounding confession of the faith, the devotion full of authority, the joy of freedom, the cry of rapture, the echo of bliss." Ambrose of Milan (c.339-397).

Isaiah 43:18-19, 21-22, 24-25   Psalm 41:1-2, 3-4, 12-13
2 Corinthians 1:18-22   Mark 2:1-12

R. *Lord, heal my soul,*
   for I have sinned against you.

Happy are those who consider the poor;
   the Lord delivers them in the day of trouble.
The Lord protects them and keeps them alive;
   they are called happy in the land.
   You do not give them up to the will of their enemies.

The Lord sustains them on their sickbed;
   in their illness you heal all of their infirmities.
As for me, I said, "O Lord, be gracious to me;
   heal me, for I have sinned against you."

But you have upheld me because of my integrity,
   and set me in your presence forever.
Blessed be the Lord, the God of Israel,
   from everlasting to everlasting.
   Amen and Amen.

The psalmist, who had been ill but was restored to health, offers thanksgiving because God continues to be merciful.

In today's gospel Jesus, to the amazement of the scribes, forgives the sins of the paralytic who was lowered through the roof by his friends. Isaiah relates the extent of God's forgiveness of sin: "your sins I remember no more." The responsorial psalm sings of a God who "sustains" us on our sickbed and who heals us from sin.

FOR THE JOURNEY

In our age of self-reliance many people find it difficult to trust others or even God. To trust means to depend on another human being or on something apart from ourselves.

And yet we often do trust others: passengers on an airplane trust the pilot; the patient trusts the surgeon and the nurses, the driver on the highway trusts the map-maker.

As choristers we need to place into our music folders a large amount of this trust: we need to trust the composer, the director, our brother and sister choir members, and—above all—the music itself, its melody and rhythm and harmony.

In a way our musical trust is a part of our overall Christian trust. The Venerable Louis Guanella once said: "I worry until midnight and from then on I let God worry."

TOOLS OF THE TRADE

Like all writers, the composers of the psalms had their own techniques, and for those of us who pray the psalms in English, perhaps the most striking of these (although not unique to Hebrew poetry) is what is known as parallelism. There are three types.

1. *Synonymous Parallelism.* Two parts of a verse repeat the same thought.

The heavens are telling the glory of God;
and the firmament proclaims his handiwork. (Ps. 19:1)

2. *Antithetical Parallelism.* The second line contrasts with the first.

The Lord watches over the way of the righteous,
but the way of the wicked will perish. (Ps 1:6)

3. *Synthetic Parallelism.* The second line builds upon the first.

He forgives all your iniquity;
he heals all your diseases. (Ps 103:3)

PRAYER

Lord God,
you spoke
and filled the darkness with light.
Open our eyes
so that we may seek you always.
Help us to hear your voice
in both the silence of our hearts
and in the wonderful sounds of all creation.

"He alone is worthy to sing psalms to the Lord, who does not utter the coarse sounds of sin, whose tongue does not blaspheme, and whose spirit is disinclined to luxury." Origen (c.185-c.254).

Hosea 2:16-17, 21-22 Psalm 103:1-2, 3-4, 8, 10, 12-13
2 Corinthians 3:1-6 Mark 2:18-22

R. *The Lord is kind and merciful.*

Bless the Lord, O my soul,
  and all that is within me
  bless his holy name.
Bless the Lord, O my soul,
  and do not forget all his benefits.

He forgives all your iniquity,
  he heals all your diseases;
he redeems your life from the pit,
  he crowns you with steadfast love and mercy.

The Lord is merciful and gracious,
  slow to anger and abounding in steadfast love.
He does not deal with us according to our sins,
  nor repay us according to our iniquities.

As far as the east is from the west,
  so far he removes our transgression from us.
As a father has compassion for his children,
  so the Lord has compassion for those who fear him.

Psalm 103 was used earlier this year, on the Seventh Sunday of Easter.

The image of God as the loving spouse is a traditional image. But Israel was often unfaithful to God. In fact, the second chapter of Hosea pictures God divorcing Israel because of the people's sins. But the chapter concludes with God leading the people out into the desert where Israel will rekindle its former love, will repent, and will again become God's spouse. The Lord is "merciful and gracious . . . abounding in kindness."

FOR THE JOURNEY

Have you ever had moments   when your life—as a human be-

64

ing, as a Christian, as a choir member—seemed to have reached a standstill? The same things over and over again. No longer any excitement, challenge, discovery. Days, weeks, and months, like a melody having neither contour nor conclusion!

Such moments are opportunities to discover parts of ourselves that we never knew existed. They offer an occasion, for instance, to enroll in a sight-singing class at a local college; or they can be an occasion to learn a keyboard or stringed instrument, to take up painting, to start a spiritual journal, to write poetry, to plant a garden, to spend a little time each week just wasting time.

The possibilities are as varied as our dreams, as far-reaching as our imaginations. But before choosing, be sure to listen, really listen, to the song in your heart.

TYPES OF PSALMS

Modern biblical scholars often sort out the psalms by categories, with some commentators discerning over ten different types.

No matter how the psalms are divided, many of them do not neatly fall into clear classifications; they are what can be called "mixed types"—their internal thought going from one category to the next, defying all efforts at compartmentalization. After all, the poet wrote from the heart and not in accord with the wishes of a commentator.

Nonetheless, knowing some of these categories will help us understand the psalms as we pray them in song. Over the next few weeks a short description of the major psalm types will be given.

PRAYER

Most loving Father,
your mercy is great,
your love without measure.
Be with us,
as your Son promised.
Sustain our song and
give gladness to our hearts.

"The community is formed in singing, assisting the blending of hearts with that of voices, eliminating differences of age, origin and social background; uniting everyone in a single aspiration of praise to God, Creator of the universe and Father of all." Paul VI, Homily (1972).

Deuteronomy 5:12-15
2 Corinthians 4:6-11

Psalm 81:2-3, 4-5, 5-7, 9-10
Mark 2:23 - 3:6 or 2:23-28

R. *Sing with joy to God our help.*

Raise a song, sound the tambourine,
  the sweet lyre with the harp.
Blow the trumpet at the new moon,
  at the full moon, on our festival day.

For it is a statute for Israel,
  an ordinance of the God of Jacob.
He made it a decree in Joseph,
  when he went out over the land of Egypt.

I hear a voice I had not known:
"I relieved your shoulder of the burden;
  your hands were freed from the basket.
In distress you called, and I rescued you."

"There shall be no strange god among you;
  you shall not bow down to a foreign god.
I am the Lord your God,
  who brought you up out of the land of Egypt.

Psalm 81 may be divided into two parts (vv. 2-6a and vv. 6b-17). The first is a short song used on the Jewish feast of Tabernacles.

Today's gospel focuses on the sabbath whose observance, Jesus says, is to benefit people since the sabbath is a day "made for humankind, and not humankind for the sabbath" (Mk 2:27). The first reading recalls God's command to observe the sabbath as a day of rest and a day in memory of the exodus from Egypt. Every Lord's Day is a call to "sing with joy to God our help."

FOR THE JOURNEY

There is a story about a young man who moved to a different city and was searching for a church to join. One Sunday he dropped into a church and, being late for the service, arrived during the sermon just as the preacher was saying: "We have left undone the things we ought to have done, and we have done those things which we ought not to have done."

The man, greatly relieved, sat down and murmured to himself "Thank God! I've found the right church at last. This is where I belong."

Thank God if we are members of a choir where we actually feel we belong. Thank God if our choir director does not allow us to leave "undone the things we ought to have done," but challenges us musically, and does so with enthusiasm, patience, and good humor.

PSALMS OF PRAISE

Praise (from the Latin *pretiare* = to prize) means to glorify, to extol, to make public the value of something or some person. It has been said that praise lies at the foundation of all Christian prayer. This is no less true of Judaism whose classic prayer type is the *berakah*. Such *berakah* blessing prayers were said at Jewish meals including the meal during which Jesus instituted the eucharist. God is blessed. God is praised.

Psalms of praise (like their *berakah* counterparts) often begin with a call or invitation to praise God, e.g., "O give thanks to the Lord" (Ps 105:1); they continue with the reason God is to be praised, e.g., God's wonders in creation, in nature, something done on behalf of the people. The psalm often concludes with another statement of praise.

For some reason most of the praise psalms occur in the second half of the psalter. They include Psalms 8, 29, 33, 98, 104, 105, 113, 117, 145, 146, 147. They are a joy to pray and a delight to sing.

PRAYER

Most merciful Father,
by the power of your Word
you have revealed to us
the image of your glory.
Nourish our hearts
with a desire for you.
Fill our songs
with the melodies of your love.

"The toiling reaper sings the psalms as he works, and the vine-dresser, as he prunes his vines, sings out one of David's songs." Origen (c.185-c.254).

Genesis 3:9-15   Psalm 130:1-2, 3-4, 5-6, 7-8
2 Corinthians 4:13 - 5:1   Mark 3:20-35

R. *With the Lord there is mercy*
   and fullness of redemption.

Out of the depths I cry to you, O Lord.
  Lord, hear my voice!
Let your ears be attentive
  to the voice of my supplications!

If you, O Lord, should mark iniquities,
  Lord, who could stand?
But there is forgiveness with you,
  so that you may be revered.

I wait for the Lord, my soul waits,
  and in his word I hope;
my soul waits for the Lord
  more than those who watch for the morning.
O Israel, hope in the Lord!

For with the Lord there is steadfast love,
  and with him is great power to redeem.
It is he who will redeem Israel
  from all its iniquities.

This psalm, a "gradual" psalm (chanted by the pilgrims as they journeyed to and from Jerusalem) and one of the most popular of the penitential psalms, requests God's mercy and forgiveness.

The grand panorama against which almost all religious traditions function is that of a struggle between the forces of good and the forces of evil. Today's first reading tells how the serpent tempted Adam in the Garden of Eden. The serpent will be conquered; good—in the end—will triumph; the Lord will overcome sin and extend forgiveness. For our part, we need to trust in God who is merciful, kind, and redeeming.

FOR THE JOURNEY

Igor Stravinsky once remarked that "religious music without religion is almost always vulgar." When he said this, he was referring to the composer. And yet this aphorism applies no less to the performer, especially to those who sing during worship.

As choir members we are first of all members of a people, a people baptized by water and the Holy Spirit, a people constantly called to conversion, a people convoked by God to hear the proclamation of the Good News (our family stories, as it were) and to share in the table fellowship of the eucharist.

Before we are a choir member, a reader, a priest, a bishop, we are Christians. This is our dignity. This is our glory . . . to be what we sing.

PSALMS OF THANKSGIVING

The God of Israel is a very personal God whose power has been brought to bear on behalf of the psalmist or the nation as a whole. There has been a bountiful harvest, the poet has been delivered or rescued from the hands of the enemy, deliverance has been given, special aid has been granted. As a result, the author expresses gratitude or gives thanks.

After a short introduction, e.g., "I will extol you, O Lord" (Ps 30:1), the poem relates the saving experience undergone by the poet or the nation. The text often concludes with a prayer for God's continuing help.

Examples of individual thanksgiving psalms are Psalms 18, 30, 32, 40, 118, 138; communal thanksgiving psalms include Psalms 34, 41, 107.

> **PRAYER**
> Almighty God,
> your love for us
> goes beyond our dreams and desires.
> Send your Spirit upon us
> so that our love for you
> may be a melody
> unsurpassed in beauty, unlike all others.

"When you are really taking part in the singing it becomes impossible to judge the total effect of the song." Joseph Gelineau, *The Liturgy Today and Tomorrow* (1978).

Ezekiel 17:22-24   Psalm 92:1-2, 12-13, 14-15
2 Corinthians 5:6-10   Mark 4:26-34

R. *Lord, it is good to give thanks to you.*

It is good to give thanks to the Lord,
   to sing praises to your name, O Most High;
to declare your steadfast love in the morning,
   and your faithfulness by night.

The righteous flourish like the palm tree,
   and grow like a cedar in Lebanon.
They are planted in the house of the Lord;
   they flourish in the courts of the Lord.

In old age they still produce fruit;
   they are always green and full of sap,
showing that the Lord is upright;
   he is my rock, and there is no unrighteousness in him.

Psalm 92, a hymn of thanksgiving, may well have been used in Jewish worship services, perhaps on the Sabbath.

This Sunday's gospel presents us with two parables: the seed that is planted and eventually results in the harvest; the small mustard seed which produces a great tree. The first reading also speaks of a tree, a cedar tree planted by God. We must never forget that every initiative on behalf of the kingdom originates with God; our own efforts, though always necessary, are of secondary importance. God remains central. "Lord, it is good to give thanks to you."

FOR THE JOURNEY

A certain amount of tension has long been part of Christianity. Does one retreat to the desert or does one serve the poor? Should the church reject the world or baptize its customs? Does God dwell in our midst or does God dwell in heaven above? And when we praise God in song, whose words are we to use?

During the years when the Christian Scriptures were being

written, the church seems to have utilized a large number of newly composed hymns, some of which were incorporated into the New Testament itself (e.g., Eph 5:19, Col 3:16, etc.) But around the year 200, a time when heretics began using hymns to propagate false doctrine, hymn singing gave way to psalmody.

In the end hymnody found a congenial home as part of the Divine Office. The Mass, on the other hand, relied heavily upon the psalter for the texts of its processional chants and the chant after the first reading.

In a sense the basic issue here is not so much God's words as opposed to human words. It is the words themselves. The words we sing and how we sing them are important, for they shape the image we have of God and of ourselves.

PSALMS OF LAMENT OR SUPPLICATION

This type of psalm springs from the "bad things" afflicting the human journey on earth. When affairs go astray, there is reason not only to complain but also to implore God's saving and compassionate aid.

Often beginning with a cry, e.g., "O Lord, how many are my foes!" (Ps 3:1), the psalmist goes on to recall either a national crisis (e.g., the destruction of Jerusalem) or a personal affliction (e.g., ridicule by enemies). Then the poem often moves to praise: God has heard and acted in the past and will do no less today.

Psalms of lament constitute the largest category of psalms in the Book of Psalms. Examples of community lament include Psalms 44, 60, 74, 79, 80; among the individual prayers of lament are Psalms 3, 5, 6, 7.

PRAYER

Lord Jesus,
you are the rising sun
giving light to our world,
dispelling the darkness of fear and sin.
Enlighten our hearts
that we may reflect
your goodness and beauty
in all that we do.

"Yonder there is no end of singing, yonder there is no end of praise . . . never will it cease, the praise of God in our Father's house." From the Welsh *Llfyr Emynau a Thonau*, tr. by H.A. Hodges.

Job 38:1, 8-11   Psalm 107:23-24, 25-26, 28-29, 30-31
2 Corinthians 5:14-17   Mark 4:35-41

R. *Give thanks to the Lord;*
  his love is everlasting.

Some went down to the sea in ships,
  doing business on the mighty waters;
they saw the deeds of the Lord,
  his wondrous works in the deep.

For he commanded and raised the stormy wind,
  which lifted up the waves of the sea.
They mounted up to the heaven,
  they went down to the depths;
  their courage melted away in their calamity.

Then they cried to the Lord in their trouble,
  and he brought them out from their distress.
he made the storm be still,
  and the waves of the sea were hushed.

Then they were glad because they had quiet,
  and he brought them to their desired haven.
Let them thank the Lord for his steadfast love,
  for his wonderful works to humankind.

Psalm 107 has two main sections: a hymn of thanksgiving (vv. 1-32) wherein the people thank Yahweh for various types of redemption; a hymn-fragment (vv. 33-43) praising God's power.

The incident of Jesus calming the waters appears in the gospel reading. And in the first reading we encounter Job. The Lord appears to Job (who was troubled by his numerous misfortunes) and declares that the very seas were created by divine power. Psalm 107 well expresses God's might and omnipotence: "he made the storm be still, and the waves of the sea were hushed."

Before the invention of music notation, people learned music by rote. One singer taught another singer or a group of singers, who in turn taught other singers. Simple melodies were not difficult to memorize, but long tunes certainly required much more time and practice. And so with the gradual appearance of a system of notation, a completely new era began.

Although we are the inheritors of this development, we often forget that the music equation is not simply that of composer-performer-listener. We need to factor in the music we hold in our hands.

We need to remember the editors, the engravers, the typesetters, the printers, and the publishers who facilitate our musical service to God's people. Their labor is no less important than our own.

WISDOM PSALMS

Wisdom (or didactic) psalms are related to the "wisdom" books of the Bible, e.g., Proverbs, Job, Sirach, etc. These psalms focus upon the deep realities of life, the serious questions confronting every thinking human being: virtuous living vs. evil living, sin and its punishment, why the wicked appear to flourish and the virtuous seem to perish.

Many of the wisdom psalms, which were not designed for liturgical use but as instruments to teach and explain how to follow God's law, contain elements common to other categories of psalms (lament).

Examples of what could be considered wisdom psalms are Psalms 25, 32, 34, 112.

PRAYER

Most powerful God,
you constantly share your love
as you lead us to the port of salvation.
Help us to live not as children of this world
but as sons and daughters
who praise your wondrous deeds
in this world and the next.

"A modest meal should sound with psalms, and if you have a good memory and a pleasant voice you should take upon yourself the singer's office." Cyprian (d.258).

Wisdom 1:13-15; 2:23-24
2 Corinthians 8:7, 9, 13-15

Psalm 30:1, 3, 4-5, 10, 11, 12
Mark 5:21-43 or 5:21-24, 35-43

R. *I will praise you, Lord,*
  for you have rescued me.

I will extol you, O Lord, for you have drawn me up,
  and did not let my foes rejoice over me.
O Lord, you brought up my soul from Sheol,
  restored me to life among those gone down to the Pit.

Sing praise to the Lord, O you his faithful ones,
  and give thanks to his holy name.
For his anger is but for a moment;
  his favor is for a lifetime.
Weeping may linger for the night,
  but joy comes with the morning.

Hear, O Lord, and be gracious to me!
  O Lord, be my helper!
You have turned my mourning into dancing.
  O Lord my God, I will give thanks to you forever.

Things had not been going well with the psalmist; he was sick, perhaps even gravely so. But God came to his aid, and thus he now offers thanks.

The gospel today relates how Jesus brought back from the dead the daughter of Jairus, one of the synagogue officials. The first reading recalls how death entered the world—through the machinations of the devil, the evil one. Yet Christ, through his death and rising, conquered death and evil. With the psalmist we can truly sing: "You have turned my mourning into dancing . . . I will give thanks to you forever."

FOR THE JOURNEY

There can be little doubt that a certain aura of mystery was connected with the pre-Vatican II Latin Mass. The use of a foreign language, the whisperings of the priest who rarely turned to look

74

at us, the atmosphere of silent adoration, the use of numerous signs of the cross and genuflections—all created a sense of the holy, of the "other," of a far-away God hidden behind the ritual.

The liturgy we celebrate today is more simple than in the recent past; it is, in fact, more classic, more reflective of the early prayer traditions of the church. Yet the very transparency of today's liturgy requires much more of the ministers than previously. More, for example, is required of presiders than merely reading the words from a book. A presider's grace, sense of communication, friendliness, his or her "feel" for the occasion can often either strengthen or weaken our prayer.

As to the choir—our posture, our appearance, the way we hold the music, the energy of our singing, are all means whereby others can find God's presence in the assembly. In a sense, we are messengers to the holy.

ROYAL PSALMS

The common element of this category of psalms is that they focus upon or are concerned with the king or the royal dynasty.

There is no uniform literary structure to these psalms which at times are placed upon the lips of the king himself, for instance, Psalms 20, 28, 61, 63, 144. At other times they are prayers for the king, e.g., on the occasion of his wedding (Ps 45), at his coronation (Ps 72 and 110), before battle (Ps 18, 21, 144), or after victory (Ps 118)

Judaism after the end of the monarchy gave all the royal psalms a messianic interpretation, whereas Christianity, in turn, applied them to Christ, who is the son of David and the "king of the Jews."

PRAYER

Lord God,
your creation delights the eye
and rejoices the ear.
Gladden our hearts
and inspire our voices,
so that we may joyfully celebrate
the wonders of your love.

"In addition to fulfilling its own proper function, the choir must be a guide and help for the congregation . . ." Cardinal J. Villot, Vatican Secretary of State (27 December 1969).

Ezekiel 2:2-5   Psalm 123:1-2, 2, 3-4
2 Corinthians 12:7-10   Mark 6:1-6

R. *Our eyes are fixed on the Lord,*
   pleading for his mercy.

To you, I lift up my eyes,
   O you who are enthroned in the heavens,
As the eyes of the servants
   look to the hand of their master.

As the eyes of a maid,
   to the hand of her mistress,
so our eyes look to the Lord our God,
   until he has mercy on us.

Have mercy upon us, O Lord,
   have mercy upon us,
   for we have had more than enough of contempt.
Our soul has had more than its fill
   of their scorn of those who are at ease,
   of the contempt of the proud.

Psalm 123 is a very short poem (only 4 verses) of supplication in which the people ask for God's mercy.

According to today's gospel the people of Jesus' home town simply could not get beyond the human elements of Our Lord's life—they simply lacked faith. And Ezekiel, when sent by God as a prophet to Israel, also encountered resistance, being unable to convert the people. We, like the people of old, need open eyes if we are to recognize and heed God's prophets in our midst.

FOR THE JOURNEY

There appears to be a good deal of ugliness, anger, and even hatred infecting the Body of Christ these days.

Various protest groups picket cathedrals and disrupt liturgies. As this book is being written, one bishop is threatening to excommunicate the "dissidents" in his diocese. A well-known television nun takes relish in declaring "There's no doubt about it, we are at war." And readers of the Letters to the Editor page in diocesan newspapers will find accusations against the "enemies" of orthodoxy, the "enemies" of Vatican II, the "enemies " of life, the "enemies" of the pope, etc.

At times such division and mistrust are even found within parish music ministries, often resulting from insecurity or empire-building.

Yet this is not the way Christ envisioned things to be. It is not the way a parish—much less a music ministry—is to "work." The words of 1 Timothy 2:8 continue to haunt us. We are told to "lift up our hands reverently in prayer, with no anger or argument." It's as simple—and at times as difficult—as that.

PSALMS OF CONFIDENCE

To place confidence in someone is to rely upon, to have faith in, to trust another person. And the psalmist, even in cases when danger or hardship is not imminent, finds it necessary to proclaim trust in God. It is a firm trust, a trust nothing can shake since God alone is the psalmist's "rock, salvation, fortress" (Ps 62:2).

In a sense these psalms are somewhat akin to psalms of lament, except that their last part is more developed.

Included among psalms of confidence are Psalms 11, 16, 23, 62, 131.

PRAYER

Lord,
creator of all that is good,
help us to be attentive
to the smallest signs
of your handiwork in creation.
Guide us, hold our hand,
as we walk with you,
as we sing of your love for people everywhere.

"If the faithful are keeping vigil in the church, David is middle and last. If at dawn any one wishes to sing hymns, David is middle and last. At funeral processions and burials, David is first, middle and last. In the holy monasteries . . . David is first, middle and last. In the convents of virgins . . . David is first, middle and last." John Chrysostom (347-407).

Amos 7:12-15
Ephesians 1:3-14 or 1:3-10

Psalm 85:8-9, 10-11, 12-13
Mark 6:7-13

R. *Lord, let us see your kindness,*
and grant us your salvation.

Let me hear what God the Lord will speak,
for he will speak peace to his people.
Surely his salvation is at hand for those who fear him
that his glory may dwell in our land.

Steadfast love and faithfulness will meet;
righteousness and peace will kiss each other.
Faithfulness will spring up from the ground,
and righteousness will look down from the sky.

The Lord will give what is good,
and our land will yield its increase.
Righteousness will go before him,
and will make a path for his steps.

This psalm, with exactly the same verses, was used once before during this liturgical year, namely, on the Second Sunday of Advent.

Today we hear of Jesus sending forth the twelve apostles to preach the need for repentance. The first reading also speaks of a mission, that of Amos—a simple shepherd lacking any formal training for his task. Yet God sent him to prophesy to the people. For our part, we must always be ready to "hear what God the Lord will speak."

FOR THE JOURNEY

Archbishop Rembert Weakland of Milwaukee once wrote that the church today cannot go back to a "golden age" of liturgical music since the composers of the past wrote for a liturgy that, in spirit and understanding, was quite different from our own.

Our liturgy, the liturgy that has resulted from Vatican II, is not only structurally more simple than the preconciliar liturgy but—and this is important for its music—is also in the vernacular and is participatory.

Although some music from the past rightfully continues to find a home in the revised liturgy, a "new song," a new repertory is also needed. And this is being developed by any number of composers, both those whose music has been published and by many more whose compositions nourish the prayer of only their own local communities.

One of our tasks and privileges as choir members is to share in the development of this new repertory. New music often requires work if it is come off the page, if it is to take on life in a community. This can only happen through our voices.

―――――――――――― THE PSALMS AS PRAYER (I) ――――――――――――

The psalms are not only inspiring religious poetry spanning almost every human emotion; they are also, and more importantly, prayers addressed to a God who, in spite of seeming absences, cares about people and who can be invoked to act on behalf of those who call upon the divine name. The God of the psalms is a close friend to whom the psalmist can expose the rawest of human emotions.

A recurring theme of the psalms is the "wonders" done by God on behalf of the poet or the people as a whole. Time and time again the Lord, never tired of insults, comes to the aid of Israel, forgives the infidelities of the people, and restores both individuals and the nation to divine favor. Similar wonders God does for us, from the day of baptism onward. We, like the psalmist, cannot help but respond with songs so full of human emotion. Whether it is praise, thanksgiving, or petition, the psalms are not only the prayerbook of Israel but also the prayerbook of the church.

PRAYER
God of faithfulness and love,
you constantly reveal yourself to us
in unexpected and wonderful ways.
Make us strong in faith,
sturdy in works,
and steadfast in prayer.

"The command to sing psalms in the name of the Lord was obeyed by everyone in every place for the command to sing is in force in all the churches which exist among the nations, not only the Greeks but also the barbarians throughout the whole world, and in towns, villages, and in the fields." Eusebius, Bishop of Caesarea (c.260-c.340).

Jeremiah 23:1-6   Psalm23:1-3, 3-4, 5, 6
Ephesians2:13-18   Mark 6:30-34

R. *The Lord is my shepherd;*
   there is nothing I shall want.

The Lord is my shepherd; I shall not want.
   He makes me to lie down in green pastures;
he leads me beside still waters;
   he restores my soul

He leads me in right paths
   for his name's sake.
Even though I walk through the darkest valley,
   I fear no evil, for you are with me;
your rod and your staff—
   they comfort me.

You prepare a table before me
   in the presence of my enemies;
you anoint my head with oil;
   my cup overflows.

Surely goodness and mercy shall follow me
   all the days of my life,
and I shall dwell in the house of the Lord
   my whole life long.

Surely the most beloved of all the psalms, Psalm 23 brings together
two themes: the figure of a shepherd who lovingly cares for his flock
and that of a host who shows generosity to the guest.

When Jesus got out of the boat, according to today's gospel, a large
crowd was waiting for him. And "he pitied them, for they were like
sheep without a shepherd." In Jeremiah we have a warning against
evil shepherds (who allow the flock to be scattered) and a promise of
good shepherds in the future. It is no surprise that today's responsorial
psalm is Psalm 23, with its lovely image of the Lord as our shepherd.

Its remote origins extend back to the ancient Romans and Greeks, but it was only in the late 1700s that the first modern one was made. In 1795 a French chemist discovered how to vary its effects, from lighter to darker. And in the mid-1800s William Monroe, a Massachusetts cabinetmaker, invented a machine that could groove and cut its external material. Not many years later, in 1861, the first U.S. factory to manufacture this object was built in New York City by Eberhard Faber.

Today more than ten million of them are produced annually throughout the world. It is, in fact, our most widely used writing and drawing instrument, namely, the lead pencil, one of the choir member's most helpful and cherished friends.

THE PSALMS AS PRAYER (II)

Christianity's love affair with the psalms already began in the early centuries of the church's existence. The reasons are many

The early members of the faithful were acutely aware that the psalms are the very word of God; they are part of the Scriptures themselves. Moreover, the psalms are also prayers on Christ's own lips and addressed to his Father.

The psalms express the voice of the church joined to Christ, its head. Additionally, the psalms are also the prayer of every disciple, whether it be the poor and the sinful or the powerful and the saintly.

The whole human condition is expressed, from the almost brutal anger of the psalmist at God's (and the psalmist's) enemies to the lofty exuberence of a voice reveling in praise of God. There is a psalm for every mood, emotion, and occasion.

> ### PRAYER
> God our Father,
> your Son has prepared a table for us
> in the celebration of the eucharist.
> Nourished by his body and blood,
> may we ever be faithful servants
> of the people
> who gather at his table.

"Good liturgies are not written; they *grow*." Dom Gregory Dix, *The Shape of the Liturgy* (1945).

2 Kings 4:42-44   Psalm 145:10-11, 15-16, 17-18
Ephesians 4:1-6   John 6:1-15

R. *The hand of the Lord feeds us;*
   he answers all our needs.

All your works shall give thanks to you, O Lord,
   and all your faithful shall bless you.
They shall speak of the glory of your kingdom,
   and tell of your power.

The eyes of all look to you,
   and you give them their food in due season.
You open your hand,
   satisfying the desire of every living thing.

The Lord is just in all his ways,
   and kind in all his doings.
The Lord is near to all who call on him,
   to all who call on him in truth.

In this psalm the poet focuses upon God's majesty and providence. Today's first lesson relates how Elisha multiplied loaves for a hundred men, whereas the gospel tells how Jesus multiplied the loaves and fishes for a vast crowd of people. Commentators often note the strong eucharistic link between this miracle and the miracle of the eucharist. It is in the eucharist that the "hand of the Lord feeds us."

FOR THE JOURNEY

There was a time, not all that long ago, when we spoke of soul and body as two distinct entities, the body being, as it were, the casing for the soul. Today this dualism has been replaced by a more biblically based concept of the unified person: there is a unity of spirit and matter, and it is by means of our bodies that we express our non-materiality.

It is through our human voices, gestures, postures, and movements that we manifest our praise of the Father. Worship on earth cannot do without the presence and action of our human bodies.

For the singer, the body is especially important. It is the basic instrument allowing us to sing. Called "a temple of the Holy Spirit" (see 1 Cor 2:16-17), the body is the singer's special gift, never to be abused by carelessness, laziness, or by addictions of any kind.

OUR MUSICAL HERITAGE

Scholarship during the present century has made us very aware of our Jewish roots, especially in regard to how we worship. At the time of Christ, Jewish worship took place (1) in the temple at Jerusalem; (2) in the various local synagogues; (3) in the home. The temple liturgy, although less influential on Christian worship than that of the synagogue or the home, is of special interest to all who sing the psalms.

The temple's musical resources were large indeed. There were singers (twelve) and instrumentalists (twelve). Although no musical artifacts from this period of Jewish history exist, we know from other evidence that the musicians played a wide variety of instruments.

The texts were primarily from the psalms and other poetic compositions. Although we don't know what the music sounded like (a clear distinction between song and speech did not yet exist), the musicians undoubtedly were capable of making a great noise to the Lord.

PRAYER

Lord God,
in Jesus you have revealed to us
the depth of your immeasurable love.
Give us our daily bread
and the bread of eternal life
so that we, nourished with divine food,
will ever remain faithful to you.

In singing the psalms "old men lay aside the rigor of age; downcast middle-aged men respond in the cheerfulness of their heart; younger men sing without peril of wantonness; youth sing without danger to their still impressionable age and without fear of being tempted to pleasure; tender maidens suffer no damage to the adornment of their chastity; and young widows let their rich voices ring out without endangering their modesty." John Chrysostom (c. 347-407).

Exodus 16:2-4, 12-15   Psalm 78:3-4, 23-24, 25, 54
Ephesians 4:17, 20-24   John 6:24-35

R. *The Lord gave them bread from heaven.*

Things that we have heard and known
  that our ancestors have told us,
We will not hide from their children;
  we will tell to the coming generation
the glorious deeds of the Lord and his might,
  and the wonders that he has done.

Yet he commanded the skies above,
  and opened the doors of heaven;
he rained down on them manna to eat,
  and gave them the grain of heaven.

Mortals ate the bread of angels;
  he sent them food in abundance.
And he brought them to his holy hill,
  to the mountain that his right hand had won.

Relatively lengthy (72 verses), Psalm 78 traces Israel's history from the Exodus to King David.

Today's liturgy of the word, like that celebrated last Sunday, has a eucharistic character. Jesus declares that "I myself am the bread of life." Exodus relates how the Jewish people, wandering in the desert and hungry, grumbled against God. Nonetheless, God rained down manna, bread from heaven, upon them.

FOR THE JOURNEY

History has used various images to describe the church, e.g., the church as the bride of Christ, as temple, as Jerusalem, etc. Perhaps the most popular and beloved of such images is the church as the "Body of Christ." The expression has its basis in Romans 12:5 ("We, though many, are one body in Christ") and in 1 Corinthians 12:27 ("You are the body of Christ, and individually members of it").

This is the image we hear at the distribution of the eucharistic bread when the minister says: "The body of Christ." Our Amen signifies that we assent to three interrelated mysteries: we acknowledge (1) that the community is the body of Christ, (2) that the communicant—by reason of water and the Holy Spirit—is the body of Christ, and (3) that the eucharistic bread is also and in a unique way the body of Christ. It is for this reason that the communion minister does not say "This is the body of Christ" or "Receive the body of Christ."

It is as the Body of Christ, and with the voice of Christ, that we give praise to the Father.

"WHAT'S THE CONNECTION?"

Have you ever noticed that at times there appears to be no direct relationship between the responsorial psalm and the readings? Well, there is a reason for this.

The compilers of the lectionary took care that when the first reading or the gospel reading cites a psalm, the quoted psalm appears as the responsory. Also, if a reading has a literary or spiritual relationship with a particular psalm, or when a particular psalm throws some light on one of the readings, then that psalm is used, e.g., Psalm 23, "The Lord Is My Shepherd," appears on the Fourth Sunday of Easter (Year A) when Christ in the gospel refers to himself as the Good Shepherd. There are also many psalms traditionally associated with certain seasons of the year, e.g. Psalms 25, 80, and 85 for Advent; Psalms 26, 51, 91, and 130 for Lent; Psalms 118 and 66 for Easter.

Finally, a certain number of psalms were simply assigned to Sundays in cases where no relationship between the reading or the season and a particular psalm could be found.

PRAYER

Most loving God,
day after day you nourish us
with the wonders of your creation.
Lead us to that heavenly banquet
where we will feast with the angels
and join them in their canticle of praise.

"After eating it is expected that everyone sing God's praises . . . whether from the holy Scriptures or out of his own talent." Tertullian (c. 160-c. 220)

1 Kings 19:4-8   Psalm 34:1-2, 3-4, 5-6, 7-8
Ephesians 4:30 - 5:2   John 6:41-51

R. *Taste and see the goodness of the Lord.*

I will bless the Lord at all times;
   his praise shall continually be in my mouth.
My soul makes its boast in the Lord;
   let the humble hear and be glad.

O magnify the Lord with me,
   and let us exult his name together.
I sought the Lord, and he answered me,
   and delivered me from all my fears.

Look to him, and be radiant;
   so your faces shall never be ashamed.
The poor soul cried, and was heard by the Lord,
   and was saved from every trouble.

The angel of the Lord encamps
   around those who fear him and delivers them.
O taste and see that the Lord is good;
   happy are those who take refuge in him.

Continuing John's discourse on the bread of life, today's gospel has Jesus explaining the statement that he is "the bread that came down from heaven." In the first reading we hear how Elijah finds a hearth cake and a jug of water. Strengthened by this food he walked forty days and forty nights to Mount Horeb. Psalm 34, a traditional eucharistic psalm, reminds us that we gather to "taste and see the goodness of the Lord."

FOR THE JOURNEY

Within recent months a number of national news magazines have featured Jesus Christ on their front covers. The accompanying feature stories often focused on contemporary attempts to discover the "historical" Jesus behind the Jesus portrayed through the faith-perspective of the Gospels.

Attempts to "figure out" God or Jesus are neither new nor unexpected. It is the nature of the human mind to probe, to discover, to stratify reality, including religious reality.

Nonetheless, Christianity is not a mathematical puzzle to be solved. It is more a dance to be joined, a landscape to be painted, a love story not only to be told but to be lived. It is the story of God being in love with us and with us falling in love with God. And people in love have, from time long ago, never hesitated to sing about it, for singing is part of the experience of love.

HYMNS DURING MASS

Vernacular singing during Mass was, from the late Middle Ages onward, a popular custom in Germany.

Already in the early seventeenth century people began to sing vernacular hymns in place of the propers (e.g., the gradual, offertory) during both high and low Masses. Although local bishops responded in various ways, the custom became deeply enrooted, especially in parish churches lacking the musical resources necessary to render the popular orchestral Masses of the day.

It was not long before such vernacular hymns also replaced the ordinary of the Mass (e.g., the *Kyrie*, the *Gloria*, etc.). Even in places where plainsong was still sung, the vernacular hymn won the day. As a result, a number of German-speaking dioceses published their own hymnals: e.g., Paderborn (1726); Speyer (1770).

And what does this have to do with us? Well, many of these local hymn books contain music we still sing today, e.g., the earliest version of the melody used for *Holy God* appears in the *Katholisches Gesang-Buch of Maria Theresa* of Austria (1774).

PRAYER

Lord Jesus,
the bread you give us
is the bread of life, the food of salvation.
Stay with us always.
Keep us always close to you
as we journey to your kingdom.

"When we pray, the voice of the heart must be heard more than the proceedings from the mouth." St. Bonaventure (1217-1284).

Proverbs 9:1-6
Ephesians 5:15-20

Psalm 34:1-2, 9-10, 11-12, 13-14
John 6:51-18

R. *Taste and see the goodness of the Lord.*

I will bless the Lord at all times;
  his praise shall continually be in my mouth.
My soul makes its boast in the Lord;
  let the humble hear and be glad.

O fear the Lord, you his holy ones,
  for those who fear him have no want.
The young lions suffer want and hunger,
  but those who see the Lord lack no good thing.

Come, O children, listen to me;
  I will teach you the fear of the Lord.
Which of you desires life,
  and covets many days to enjoy good?

Keep your tongue from evil,
  and your lips from speaking deceit.
Depart from evil, and do good;
  seek peace, and pursue it.

Psalm 34 was also used as last Sunday's responsorial psalm, although—for the most part—with different verses.

The gospel today continues with Jesus explaining that he is the bread from heaven. Proverbs speaks about the meal that Wisdom offers to her followers. It is a sumptuous repast to which the guests are invited: "Come, eat of my food, and drink of the wine I have mixed." In a sense this invitation prefigures the invitation Christ extends to us at every eucharistic celebration. When we respond, we—like those who see God—"lack no good thing."

FOR THE JOURNEY

God's wonders in creation have long been a point of departure for spiritual writers. The majesty of the mountain peak, the refreshing coolness of the flowing stream, the breathtaking hues of the rainbow, the fragile beauty of the violet—all are among the most wonderful and beautiful works of God.

And yet as beautiful as all creation is, we—made in God's very likeness and image—are the most beautiful. God's special favor rests upon us. What we do, what we say, what we sing, all are filled with the breath of God, with God's Spirit. This is our glory, and for this we, unique among all creation, sing thanks.

"THE FATHER OF LATIN HYMNODY"

Certainly one of the church's greatest bishops is St. Ambrose of Milan (c.340-397). While he was still a catechumen, the people by popular acclaim nominated him to be bishop of Milan. After some hesitation Ambrose consented. He was then baptized and ordained. Influential in the conversion of St. Augustine (386), Ambrose was noted as an author, a preacher, and as a very pastorally minded bishop.

He was also a strong promoter of congregational singing. When surrounded by the Arian soldiers of the emperor Valentinian II, Ambrose had his flock gather with him in the Milan cathedral where they supported one another through common song. This great churchman, we are told, introduced antiphonal singing (two choirs alternating verses) in Milan and was himself the composer of a number of Latin hymn texts and is known as the "Father of Latin Hymnody."

The feast of St. Ambrose is celebrated on December 7th.

PRAYER

Lord God,
you have created the earth and the heavens
out of love for us.
You have shared your life with us
in the person of Jesus Christ.
Bring our hearts ever closer to you
as we celebrate your name in song.

"What a grand bond of unity becomes clearly evident when a multitude of diverse people sing in unison! Like a harp with many strings sounding a single melody! The fingers of a musician may strike wrong chords at times, but not here—for among God's people it is his Spirit who is the master-musician." Ambrose of Milan (c.339-397).

89

Joshua 24:1-2, 15-17, 18   Psalm 34:1-2, 15-16, 17-18, 19-20, 21-22
Ephesians 5:21-32   John 6:60-69

R. *Taste and see the goodness of the Lord.*

I will bless the Lord at all times;
  his praise shall continually be in my mouth.
My soul makes its boast in the Lord;
  let the humble hear and be glad.

The eyes of the Lord are on the righteous,
  and his ears are open to their cry.
The face of the Lord is against evildoers,
  to cut off the remembrance of them from the earth.

When the righteous cry for help, the Lord hears,
  and rescues them from all their troubles.
The Lord is near to the brokenhearted,
  and saves the crushed in spirit.

Many are the afflictions of the righteous,
  but the Lord rescues them from them all.
He keeps all their bones;
  not one of them will be broken.

Evil brings death to the wicked,
  and those who hate the righteous will be condemned.
The Lord redeems the life of his servants;
  none of those who take refuge in him will be condemned.

This Sunday we finish Christ's discourse on the bread of life. As the gospel selection ends, the disciples, realizing what a difficult teaching Jesus was presenting, refused to "remain in his company any longer." The Twelve, however, remained faithful. The reading from Joshua also has the people facing a choice. He tells the tribes of Israel to "decide today whom you will serve." And when we gather for the eucharist, we too are faced with a choice since the eucharist demands that our whole lives—especially what we do after Mass—"bless the Lord at all times."

Mr. O'Brien, a dynamic and enthusiastic bass, had a dream in which he was singing in a choir having a thousand sopranos, a thousand altos, and a thousand tenors. He was the only bass. The choir was singing along just fine and had reached a double forte when the conductor suddenly stopped the singing by rapping on his music stand and re-marked, "Mr. O'Brien, a little less volume on the bass part, please."

Few of us have voices like that. But all of us could use at least a little of his confidence. We need to sing as though everything depends on us, as indeed it does.

— HYMNS AND HYMNALS, PROTESTANT AND CATHOLIC —

Hymnals have a long and varied history in the Christian Church. Already in the early Middle Ages the Latin hymns used for the Divine Office were collected into books called "hymnaries" (*Libri Hymnarii*), the earliest of these without musical notation and later on (twelfth and thirteenth centuries) with melodies completely written out.

The Protestant Reformation in Germany (especially Martin Luther) emphasized congregational singing, and so the sixteenth century saw the publication of a large number of Lutheran hymnals.

In the U.S. the first collection of music for Catholic church services, and the remote ancestor of our present hymnals, was John Aitken's *A Compilation of the Litanies and Vespers Hymns and Anthems as they are sung in the Catholic Church adapted for the Voice and Organ,* published in Philadelphia (1787). The title indicates the diverse nature of the volume; texts were in Latin, English, and German. A few copies can still be found in research libraries today.

PRAYER

Most powerful God,
you never fail to rescue us
from dangers of all kind.
Help us today and each day of our lives
so that we may always use well
the many gifts you have given us.

"Hymns breathe the praise of the saints,
the vision of the prophets,
the prayers of the penitent and the spirit of the martyrs." Anon.

91

Deuteronomy 4:1-2, 6-8   Psalm 15:2-3, 3-4, 4-5
James 1:17-18, 21-22, 27   Mark 7:1-8, 14-15, 21-23

R. *He who does justice will live in the presence of the Lord.*

Those who walk blamelessly, and do what is right,
  and speak the truth from their heart,
  who do not slander with their tongue.

Those who do no evil to their friends,
  nor take up a reproach against their neighbor;
in whose eyes the wicked are despised,
  but who honor those who fear the Lord.

Those who do not lend money at interest,
  and do not take a bribe against the innocent.
Those who do these things
  shall never be disturbed.

Here the psalmist enumerates certain moral qualities required for admittance to the temple.

Jesus in today's gospel insists that the human heart is defiled only by what comes from within a person. The reading from Deuteronomy recalls that the commandments are a sign of God's enduring love for us. For our part, when we walk in the way of God's law, we "live in the presence of the Lord . . . (we) shall never be disturbed."

FOR THE JOURNEY

It is obvious that the church's worship involves more than a series of prayers recited one after another. Words, it is true, are part of the fabric of our liturgy but other elements (e.g., gesture, posture, action, movement, etc.) are no less integral to this fabric. In addition, there is a dynamic, an ebb and a flow, as to how all these elements are woven together. There are strong moments (e.g., the eucharistic prayer) and more relaxed moments (e.g., the preparation of the gifts). There are times to speak, to listen, to sing, to respond, and yes, to be silent.

Silence does not come easily to us choir members; after all, we are there to sing. (The problem seems to be shared with many presiders.) Silence is not efficient, and we live in an age of efficiency. Furthermore, as Roman Catholics most of us were not raised with a tradition of silence.

Nonetheless, to participate in silence is to put aside all cares. It is a time to do nothing other than to listen for the voice of God, the God whose voice is, perhaps, most often heard not in the stirring strains of an Alleluia but in the silent hush of a quiet whisper.

HYMNAL OR SERVICE BOOK?

Church musicians today often speak about service books rather than hymnals. Is there a difference? Strictly speaking, a hymnal is primarily a collection of hymns, and so in the U.S. we had the *St. Gregory Hymnal and Choir Book*, the *St. Mary's Hymnal*, and others.

But with Vatican II's reform of the liturgy, publishers came to realize that people, to participate musically, need more in a book than just a collection of hymns. Thus the traditional hymnal soon began to evolve and include not only hymns but also music for the complete Order of Mass (blessing and sprinkling of holy water, penitential rite, *Gloria*, antiphons for responsorial psalmody, etc.), music for the liturgy of the hours and various sacramental celebrations, various prayers, introductions to and commentaries on the various rites.

This type of book, is often referred to as a service book. Furthermore, the old Roman Catholic hymnal was in most communities more of a "choir" book, whereas a service book is designed to assist the participation of the people at large.

PRAYER

Lord Jesus,
you walked among us
as our friend and brother.
Stay with us always,
keep us close to you,
and present our gift of song
to the Father.

"In the liturgy, music, like all other ritual activity, must first be thought of in terms of the people who are celebrating." Universa Laus, *Points of Reference*, no. 3.1.

Twenty-Third Sunday of the Year

Isaiah 35:4-7   Psalm 146:5-7, 8-9. 9-10
James 2:1-5   Mark 7:31-37

R. *Praise the Lord, my soul!*

Happy are those whose help is the God of Jacob,
   who keeps faith forever,
   who executes justice for the oppressed,
   who give food to the hungry.
The Lord sets the prisoners free.

The Lord opens the eyes of the blind.
The Lord lifts up those who are bowed down;
   the Lord loves the righteous.
The Lord watches over the strangers.

He upholds the orphan and the widow,
   but the way of the wicked he brings to ruin.
The Lord will reign forever,
   your God, O Zion, for all generations.
Praise the Lord.

In this poem, the first of the Alleluia Psalms (Ps 146-150) which conclude the psalter, the author praises God's greatness and goodness.

According to Isaiah the coming of the Messiah will be accompanied
by many wonderful things, including the opening of the eyes of the
blind and the clearing of the ears of the deaf. The gospel today relates
an incident of the latter: Jesus "put his fingers in the man's ears . . .
(and) said to him 'Ephphatha' . . . (and) the man's ears were opened."
The people, we are told, were dumbstruck by this: "Their amazement
went beyond all bounds." Similar miracles continue today, and so with
the psalmist we sing: "Praise the Lord, my soul."

FOR THE JOURNEY

One of the unique characteristics of worship is that we have to
do it ourselves. We cannot send
someone else to take our place.
There can be no substitutes. Liturgy, as the "work of the peo-

94

ple," requires an assembly of believers who use their own voices, who sit, stand, and kneel, who physically engage in a common action, who carry out human signs in a human way.

It is for this reason that the human voice upraised in song permits no stand-ins at worship, even when such is possible due to modern day technology. To quote the U.S. bishops: "Record- ed music . . . should, as a general norm, never be used within the liturgy to replace the congregation, the choir, the organists or other instrumentalists (*Liturgical Music Today*, no. 60).

As beautiful as a piece of music might sound on a CD, it can never equal the sound of a living voice which, in its own unique way, mirrors the voice of the living God.

POETRY IN A CAVE?

History, including the history of Christian hymnody, is haunted by myth and legend.

In Germany there is a little town called Mettman. Its literary hero is Joachim Neander (1650-1680), one of Germany's greatest hymn text writers. The locals take delight in pointing out a nearby cave where, they will tell you, Neander took refuge after having problems with church authorities. And it was here, they say, that he wrote his poetry.

Neander, converted to the Lord after having heard a sermon in church, was a minister and school administrator, and he did encounter difficulties with his ecclesiastical superiors (nothing new here), but there is no evidence that he wrote any poetry in a cave.

What is certain is that one of his poems, published the year of his death, was soon sung to a traditional folk-like tune, and both text and melody have come down to us: *Praise to the Lord, the Almighty.*

PRAYER

O God our Father,
you constantly shield us
with your love and protection.
Continue to watch over us.
Remove all dangers,
and guide us through the work at hand.

"To participate intelligently in liturgical worship is now to participate actively in the reform of the whole Church." Thomas Merton, *Seasons of Celebration* (1965).

Isaiah 50:4-9
James 2:14-18

Psalm 116:1-2, 3-4, 5-6, 8-9
Mark 8:27-35

R. *I will walk in the presence of the Lord,
     in the land of the living.*

I love the Lord because he has heard
     my voice and my supplications.
Because he has inclined his ear to me.

The snares of death encompassed me;
     the pangs of Sheol laid hold on me;
I suffered distress and anguish.
Then I called on the name of the Lord:
     "O Lord, I pray, save my life."

Gracious is the Lord and righteous;
     our God is merciful.
The Lord protects the simple;
     when I was brought low, he saved me.

For you have delivered my soul from death,
     my eyes from tears, my feet from stumbling.
I will walk before the Lord
     in the land of the living.

Psalm 116 was used earlier this year—on the Second Sunday of Lent—as the responsorial psalm.

Today Peter affirms that Jesus is the Messiah. And then, according to Mark, Jesus began to teach the disciples "that the Son of Man had to suffer much, be rejected . . . be put to death." The selection from Isaiah stands in relation to Christ's prediction of his Passion, and yet there is hope of victory: the Lord has "delivered my soul from death, my eyes from tears, my feet from stumbling."

FOR THE JOURNEY

Anyone who has ever attended a convention of church musi- cians knows that pastoral music is big business. The exhibit hall finds music publishers, large and small, selling their recent releases. Composers are demonstrating their latest compositions. Thousands and thousands of dollars are involved. It is business and big business at that. It is a land of "big bucks." We should be neither surprised nor shocked. And yet this is not "where it's at."

Pastoral music is found gently carried in the hands and voices of those numerous singers, directors, and instrumentalists who bring musical prayer to life in countless communities throughout the country. They do so without fanfare, with dedication, and with love. No great fortunes to be made here, no fortune at all unless that given in another land.

"WATTS' WHIMS"

Whether it's an Anglican, Methodist, or Roman Catholic hymn or service book, you're sure to find one or more texts by Isaac Watts (1674-1748), who has been called the "Father of English Hymnody."

Born in Southampton, England, Watts was a gifted child, learning Latin at the age of 5, Greek at 9, French at 11, and Hebrew at 12. Not a member of the state Anglican Church, he became an independent (Congregationalist) minister. At that time churches favored psalm singing, and so Watts was asked by his father to "write something better for us to sing." He did so, writing some six hundred "humanly composed" hymns and psalm paraphrases, yet not without opposition. Those who objected called these texts "Watts' Whims."

Among his best-known texts are *Joy to the World* and *O God, Our Help in Ages Past*.

PRAYER

Lord God,
your wisdom exceeds all understanding.
Your love for us makes no exceptions.
Listen to our prayers,
cleanse our hearts,
and bless whatever we do
in the name of Jesus.

"Music in worship must be true art. If we today keep that standard high, we will be preparing in the best way possible for tomorrow." Rembert Weakland, O.S.B., *Themes of Renewal* (1995).

Wisdom 2:17-20 Psalm 54:1-2, 3, 4-6
James 3:16 - 4:3 Mark 9:30-37

> R. *The Lord upholds my life.*
>
> Save me, O God, by your name,
>   and vindicate me by your might.
> Hear my prayer, O God;
>   give ear to the words of my mouth.
>
> For the insolent have risen against me,
>   the ruthless seek my life;
>   they do not set God before them.
>
> But surely, God is my helper;
>   the Lord is the upholder of my life.
> With a freewill offering I will sacrifice to you;
>   I will give thanks to your name, O Lord, for it is good.

In this very short poem the psalmist requests God's help and then promises a thanksgiving sacrifice.

Today Christ again predicts his Passion: "The Son of Man is going to be delivered into the hands of men who will put him to death." The Old Testament reading prefigures Christ's fate: as the wicked say, "Let us condemn him to a shameful death." And the responsorial psalm makes us think of both Calvary and the Resurrection.

FOR THE JOURNEY

Certainly the most prolific American hymn text writer was Fanny J. Crosby (1820-1915) who composed over eight thousand hymn texts. Although Fanny was blind from six weeks of age due to improper medical treatment, she was always optimistic, joyful, confident, and even rejoiced in her blindness because, she said, "when I get to heaven, the first sight that shall ever gladden my eyes will be that of my Savior."

One of her famous hymns is *My Savior First of All*, which contains the lines: "O the dear ones in glory, how they beckon me to come . . . to the sweet vale of

98

Eden they will sing my welcome home."

We need only think of our ancestors in the faith, our own family members, and perhaps even those who were once so much a part of our choir, all who have gone before us to that wondrous garden, to that eternal Jerusalem, where "they will sing" our "welcome home." What a song that will be! What a day!

_____"THAT SAVED A WRETCH LIKE ME"_____

As a youth he was pressed into naval service. According to his own testimony, all types of debauchery followed. Eventually becoming a slave-trader, he transported men, women, and children from Africa to slave markets around the world. Then one day, caught up in a terrible ocean storm, he began to read *The Imitation of Christ* by Thomas à Kempis. Converted on March 10, 1748, he studied for the ministry, was ordained in the Anglican Church, and was appointed curate at Olney, a village near Cambridge in England. To assist his preaching he wrote hymns renowned for their directness, simplicity, and lack of pretense. His name was Newton, not Isaac Newton the scientist, but John Newton (1725-1807), curate, poet, and letter writer.

The thought of such a degenerate past life so overwhelmed him that Newton, in his poetry, could refer to grace as having saved "a wretch like me." A strong word, indeed, and one that makes us somewhat uncomfortable. Yet this was the term Newton employed to describe the human condition before Christ's saving action. Many of the hymns we sing today carry with them a poet's theological outlook or auto-biographical wrapping. *Amazing Grace* is no exception.

PRAYER

All-powerful and ever-living God,
you are the font of all holiness,
the source of all that is good.
Help us to be faithful in doing your work.
May our song always be that of Christ,
our harvest be one of justice and love.

"Christianity is not a theory or speculation, but a life; not a philosophy of life, but a living presence. This realization can turn any gloom into a song." Samuel Taylor Coleridge (1772-1834).

Numbers 11:25-29   Psalm 19:7, 9, 11-12, 13
James 5:1-6   Mark 9:38-43, 45, 47-48

R. *The precepts of the Lord give joy to the heart.*

The law of the Lord is perfect,
　　reviving the soul;
the decrees of the Lord are sure,
　　making wise the simple.

The fear of the Lord is pure,
　　enduring forever;
The ordinances of the Lord are true
　　and righteous altogether.

Moreover by them is your servant warned;
　　in keeping them there is great reward.
But who can detect their errors?
　　Clear me from hidden faults.

Keep back your servant also from the insolent;
　　do not let them have dominion over me.
Then I shall be blameless,
　　and innocent of great transgression.

Psalm 19 was used this year on the Third Sunday of Lent.

Today's gospel touches upon a number of points, e.g., the casting out of demons by people who are not disciples, giving scandal to the "little ones," and finally, avoiding sin at all costs. Through baptism we become sharers in God's kingdom, and our calling is to observe the standards of this kingdom. God's law is a positive law to be followed with loving devotion. "The law of the Lord is perfect, reviving the soul."

FOR THE JOURNEY

Several years ago I was participating in a local parish's Sunday liturgy. After the distribution of the eucharist the choir—located in a loft at the back of the building—sang a motet and did so very well. When the singing concluded, the people stood up, turned toward the loft, and began to clap. Something terribly wrong, I believe, was happening here.

Certainly there is nothing amiss with showing appreciation to the choir (there are appropriate ways and times to do this). Yet communion is the time when we should be applauding Jesus, who brought about our salvation, who has entered our hearts, and through whom we, as one people, offer praise to God our Father.

"AMAZING GRACE"

Someone once said that a memorable hymn results from the marriage of a text that stirs the soul with a melody that stirs the voice. Needed are lyrics everyone can relate to and a tune everyone can sing. And this is what we have in Newton's *Amazing Grace*.

John Newton wrote this six stanza poem (it originally had the awkward title of *Faith's Review and Expectations*) sometime before 1779. Yet it took almost 120 years before the text met the melody we sing today.

The tune (called ANDERSON, CHALMERS, FRUGALITY, HARMONY, HARMONY GROVE, NEW BRITAIN, etc.), though with various texts, first began to appear in U.S. hymn collections as early as 1829. Some music historians believe it derives from a secular Scottish air. At any rate, in 1900 Edwin Excell, a Chicago publisher, joined Newton's poetry to the now familiar melody. Certainly, a marriage made in heaven.

Though long popular among fundamentalist congregations, only recently has *Amazing Grace* entered the hymnals of many mainline churches.

PRAYER

God our Father,
you give us your Son
as your Word
dwelling among us.
Grant that we, with him,
may ever acclaim your wonders
and laud your name.

"Who hears music, feels his solitude peopled at once." Robert Browning (1812-1889), *Balaustion's Adventure*.

Genesis 2:18-24   Psalm 128:1-2, 3, 4-5, 6
Hebrews 2:9-11   Mark 10:2-16 or 10:2-12

R. *May the Lord bless us*
   all the days of our lives.

Happy is everyone who fears the Lord,
   who walks in his ways.
You shall eat the fruit of the labor of your hands;
   you shall be happy, and it shall go well with you.

Your wife will be like a fruitful vine
   within your house;
your children will be like olive shoots
   around your table.

Thus shall the man be blessed
   who fears the Lord.
The Lord bless you from Zion.
May you see the prosperity of Jerusalem
   all the days of your life.

May you see your children's children,.
   Peace be upon Israel.

Psalm 128, which may have been sung by the pilgrims on their journey to Jerusalem, celebrates the joys of family life.

In today's gospel Jesus, responding to the Pharisees, insists on the fidelity required of the man and the woman who are united in marriage. Jesus quotes from Genesis: "for this reason a man shall leave his father and mother and the two shall become as one."

At a time when marriage seems to be threatened from many quarters, we pray that God bless husbands and wives, that God bless all parents.

FOR THE JOURNEY

A few years ago a book was published which caused quite a stir in church music circles. Entitled *Why Catholics Can't Sing*, its author is professor at an East Coast college.

The book, well-written, often witty, and occasionally quite insightful, is generally unsympathetic to what has happened musically in the church since Vatican II. At times, unfortunately, the author is simply mean-spirited. He could have profited from the services of a wise editor.

The publishers have supplied an index, and indexes reveal so much. "Vatican II" receives four entries. "Prayer" receives not a single entry.

"FAITH OF OUR FATHERS"

Frederick William Faber (1814-1863) was one of the most prolific hymn text writers of the nineteenth century. Ordained in the Church of England but eventually—under the influence of the Oxford Movement—becoming a Roman Catholic, Faber's goal was to give an impetus to hymn singing among Catholics in the British Isles.

He wrote two versions of *Faith of Our Fathers*, one for the conversion of England, the other for Ireland. The third stanza of that for England contained the lines "Mary's prayers / shall bring" as well as "England shall . . . be free." So powerful was Faber's poetry that even Protestant hymnals began to include the text, but the wording had to be "purified." Thus already in 1853 the Unitarian hymnal contained this hymn but with the following changes: "God's great power / shall bring" and "Mankind shall . . . be free." Nonetheless, Christians of all denominations share a faith which has come down to us from the past. And music remains a primary place where we can express this common heritage.

PRAYER

Lord God,
you created us to be your family,
to be a city at peace,
to be a people in love with you.
Help us to love you above all things
so that our melody
may always ascent from hearts
ever free from sin.

"God gave me a cheerful heart, so he will surely forgive me if I serve him cheerfully." Franz Joseph Haydn (1732-1809).

Twenty-Eighth Sunday of the Year

Wisdom 7:7-11
Hebrews 4:12-13

Psalm 90:12-13, 14-15, 16-17
Mark 10:17-30 or 10:17-27

R. *Fill us with your love, O Lord,*
  and we will sing for joy!

Teach us to count our days
  that we may gain a wise heart.
Turn, O Lord! How long?
  Have compassion on your servants!

Satisfy us in the morning with your steadfast love,
  so that we may rejoice and be glad all our days.
Make us glad as many days as you have afflicted us.

Let your work be manifest to your servants,
  and your gracious power to their children.
Let the favor of the Lord our God be upon us,
  and prosper for us the work of our hands—
  O prosper the work of our hands!

Psalm 90 reflects upon the transitory nature of our existence: God's days last forever; human life upon earth comes to an end.

In today's gospel Jesus warns against being attached to this world: "How hard it is for the rich to enter the kingdom of God!" The first reading tells us that to be truly wise is to be rich indeed. And it is for a "wise heart" that we pray in today's psalm.

FOR THE JOURNEY

In the tenth century Prince Vladimir of Kiev was besieged by the Moslems, by the Latin rite Catholics, by the Jews, and by the Orthodox from Constantinople. Each group wanted Vladimir to adopt their particular faith as the official religion of Rus.

Legend has it that the Prince received the following advice from his counselors: "You know that no man condemns his own possessions, but praises them instead. If you desire to make certain, you have servants at your disposal. Send them to inquire about the ritual of each and how each worships God."

Note that the servants were sent out to evaluate liturgy and not theological formulation. Despite the importance of the latter, how we celebrate and what we celebrate says more about ourselves than all the books found on all the shelves of our libraries.

And, by the way, it is in Constantinople that the Russian Orthodox Church has its roots.

"HOLY GOD"

In pre-Vatican II years a sure way to get the people (including the members of the Holy Name Society) to sing at the end of a service was to conclude with *Holy God.* Along with Friday abstinence and memorizing the catechism, it was a sign of being a Catholic.

We owe the English words of this hymn to an American priest with the elegant name of Clarence Alphonsus Walworth (1820-1900), who studied theology at the General Theological Seminary in New York City. Walworth soon converted to Roman Catholicism, continued his studies in Belgium and Holland, and was ordained in 1848.

During his stay in Europe Walworth, while visiting Germany, became acquainted with a German metrical version of the ancient Latin hymn *Te Deum.* He translated the German, and the translation was included in a Redemptorist mission manual (c. 1850). Within a few years the text was linked to a melody first found in an Austrian Catholic hymnal dating from about 1774.

Walworth eventually left the Redemptorists, for a time was associated with the Paulist Fathers, and then served for many years as pastor of St. Mary's parish in Albany, NY.

PRAYER

God our Father,
you wisdom is inscrutable,
your love without bounds.
Take charge of our voices
so that your songs
may fill our days with gladness
and help us overcome
the perils of the night.

"The aim and final reason for all music should be nothing else but the glory of God and the refreshment of the spirit." J. S. Bach (1685-1750).

Twenty-Ninth Sunday of the Year

Isaiah 53:10-11
Hebrews 4:14-16

Psalm 33:4-5, 18-19, 20-22
Mark 10:35-45 or 10:42-45

R. *Lord, let your mercy be on us,*
  as we place our trust in you.

The word of the Lord is upright,
  and all his work is done in faithfulness.
He loves righteousness and justice;
  the earth is full of the steadfast love of the Lord.

Truly the eye of the Lord is on those who fear him,
  on those who hope in his steadfast love,
to deliver their soul from death,
  and to keep them alive in famine.

Our soul waits for the Lord;
he is our help and shield.
Let your steadfast love, O Lord, be upon us,
  even as we hope in you.

Psalm 33 was used previously this year, on Trinity Sunday.

Today's first reading as well as the gospel present us with the Suffering Servant who "through his suffering shall justify many, and their guilt he shall bear"; and Jesus who "has not come to be served but to serve—to give his life in ransom for the many." To suffer and die is part of the human condition. Nonetheless, death is not final; the Lord is "our help and shield" in whom "we place our trust."

FOR THE JOURNEY

Almost twenty years ago there appeared a wonderful booklet, *Persons in Liturgical Celebrations*, by Lucien Deiss, in which he explains various ministries.

Often we think of ministries in terms of the people at large, the community, the assembly being served. But there is another aspect, one we often overlook. To quote Father Deiss: "Who renders the best service or ministry to the community: the priest who gives a marvelous homily which inflames all the hearts or the little old lady who does not understand anything but prays her rosary softly and whose heart is an immense brazier of love? The sick person who . . . offers himself in sacrifice to the Lord or the organist who makes the little girls shiver and the old people turn their heads by starting the *Toccata in D Minor* of Johann Sebastian Bach? The soprano with the golden voice who puts all her soul into hitting the high notes . . . or the little boy who sings awry but in whom the angels—it is said in the Gospel—contemplate without ceasing the face of the Father? No one would know how to decide. No one knows the scale of the Good Lord. For the angels place on the scale not what appears in liturgy, but the weight of each heart, the weight of love."

"JOYFUL, JOYFUL, WE ADORE THEE"

In 1907 Henry van Dyke (1852-1933), a Presbyterian minister, was visiting Williams College in Williamstown, MA. One morning at breakfast he gave a poem he had just written to the college president, James Garfield, and said: "Here is a hymn for you. Your mountains (the Berkshires) were my inspiration. It must be sung to the tune of Beethoven's 'Hymn to Joy'." And so it was that *Joyful, Joyful, We Adore Thee* came to be written, and within a few years was actually paired with Beethoven's stirring melody.

Henry van Dyke also taught English literature at Princeton University, was our country's minister to Holland and Luxembourg, and served as a chaplain in the U.S. Navy.

PRAYER

Lord God,
you look upon us
with mercy and love.
Help us to place our trust in you alone
so that our voices may confidently
announce your wonders
and proclaim your goodness.

"Good celebrations foster and nourish faith. Poor celebrations weaken and destroy faith." Bishops' Committee on the Liturgy, *Music in Catholic Worship*, no. 6 (1972).

Jeremiah 31:7-9
Hebrews 5:1-6

Psalm 126:1-2, 2-3, 4-5, 6
Mark 10:46-52

R. *The Lord has done great things for us;*
  we are filled with joy.

When the Lord restored the fortunes of Zion,
  we were like those who dream.
Then our mouth was filled with laughter,
  and our tongues with shouts of joy.

Then it was said among the nations,
  "The Lord has done great things for them."
The Lord has done great things for us,
  and we rejoiced.

Restore our fortunes, O Lord,
  like the watercourses in the Neg'eb.
May those that sow in tears
  reap with shouts of joy.

Those who go out weeping.
  bearing seed for sowing,
shall come home with shouts of joy,
  carrying their sheaves.

Psalm 126 is the song of the returned exiles who not only recall God's past deeds but who ask that divine help again be granted.

Today we hear of Christ giving sight to the blind beggar sitting by the roadside. The first reading says that the Lord will bring back the exiles "with the blind and the lame in their midst." Continuing this thought, the psalm sings of the great things the Lord did for the Jews of old and for us today. "We are filled with joy."

FOR THE JOURNEY

A liturgical architect simply has to design a beautiful and functional church building. An organ builder simply has to build an organ that serves the purposes of the community. The artisan simply has to fashion attractive vestments, vessels, and other accouterments necessary for worship. All these individuals are judged on the basis of their products.

It is quite another matter for those engaged in ministry. These men and women must, before all else, share the Christian faith, must be committed to the church and the values the church holds dear, must have entered into a relationship with the Lord.

Like all who serve the community, choir members must constantly become more Christian. Day after day we must undertake the work of conversion, that "change of heart" preached by Jesus and the apostles. Conversion, like learning an unfamiliar tune, takes time and labor. But the result, in both cases, is a new creation, a new song.

DESIGN OR COINCIDENCE?

One of the church's best-known Trinitarian hymns is *Holy, Holy, Holy! Lord God Almighty*.

The text's author was an Englishman, the Anglican bishop Reginald Heber (1783-1826), who served for a time as the Bishop of Calcutta. Shortly after his death a collection of his poems was published; it included this hymn.

In 1860 John Bacchus Dykes (1823-1876), the chief musician at Durham Cathedral, wrote a melody for Heber's text; it proved a success and was called NICAEA, the name of the ancient city that played a major part in formulating early doctrine on the Trinity.

The melody is stately, noble, easily remembered. But did you ever notice that the tune begins with intervals of a third? By design or coincidence?

PRAYER

Lord God,
you lift us up when we fall,
you gladden our hearts when they are sad.
Continue to do great things for us.
Help us to sing rather than weep,
to walk straight rather than stumble.
Be with us, Lord.

"Our tunes are . . . left to the mercy of every unskillful throat to chop and alter, twist and change, according to their infinitely diverse and no less odd humours and fancies." Thomas Walter (1696-1725).

Deuteronomy 6:2-6
Hebrews 7:23-28

Psalm 18:1-2, 2-3, 46, 50
Mark 12:28-34

R. *I love you, Lord, my strength.*

I love you, O Lord, my strength.
The Lord is my rock, my fortress, and my deliverer.

My God, my rock in whom I take my refuge,
  my shield, and the horn of my salvation,
  my stronghold.
I call upon the Lord, who is worthy to be praised,
  so I shall be saved from my enemies.

The Lord lives! Blessed be my rock,
  and exalted be the God of my salvation.
Great triumphs he gives to his king,
  and shows steadfast love to his anointed.

Psalm 18, attributed to David and actually placed on David's lips in 2 Samuel 22, is a thanksgiving poem for help and victory. It pictures God as the great master of creation.

To love God and to love one's neighbor are, according to Jesus in today's gospel, the two great commandments. In answering the scribe as to which is the first of the commandments, Jesus begins by quoting Deuteronomy: "The Lord is our God, the Lord alone! Therefore you shall love the Lord . . ." Using the text of Psalm 18, one of the few psalms that employ the word "love" with God as its object, we sing: "I love you, Lord, my strength."

FOR THE JOURNEY

There is a group of psalms that might be called "nature" psalms. In these poems the poet calls upon all creation to join in the offering of praise: the sun and the moon, the stars, the fire and hail, the waters, the mountains and hills, the snow and the rain, the birds and the cattle—and yes, even the reptiles.

Psalms of this kind are usually very melodic and rhythmic and so are fun to sing. But they require more than singing. There is another element that, in our musical exuberance, we can too easily overlook. We must never forget that, once the singing is over, the earth—and indeed all creation, all God's garden—must be treated gently, with compassion, with reverence.

"PRAYER AFTER MEALS"

It has been suggested that *Now Thank We All Our God* is the most widely-known hymn of all time. Whether such a claim is true or not, all would agree it is a classic.

The lyrics were written by Martin Rinkart (1585-1649), a Lutheran who was cantor and subsequently deacon at Eisleben in Germany, then pastor at Ardeborn, and finally archdeacon of Eilenburg.

This was a very sad period of history: the plague of 1637 had carried off some five thousand people (including Rinkart's wife); the Thirty Years War was still raging. And yet it appears that the lyrics were written not in light of major societal worries but for domestic use. The text, composed about 1630, apparently was intended for Rinkart's children to sing as a prayer after meals. Within a short time it was sung to a strong melody by Johann Crüger (1598-1663), a noted Lutheran composer who was music director at St. Nicholaus church in Berlin.

Our beautiful translation of the text is the work of Catherine Winkworth (1827-1878), an English lady who provided numerous English translations of German hymnody. But it was not till after the Second Vatican Council that the hymn became common in American Catholic churches, an ecumenical gesture which enriches us so greatly.

PRAYER

O God,
Creator of the universe,
you protect us from evils of every kind.
Help us to love you
and to take delight in you.
May our voices be filled
with the joy that comes from you alone.

"One cannot find anything more religious and more joyful in sacred celebrations than a whole congregation expressing its faith . . . in song."
Sacred Congregation of Rites, Instruction *Musicam Sacram*, no. 16 (1967).

1 Kings 17:10-16   Psalm 146:6, 7-8, 8-9
Hebrews 9:24-28   Mark 12:38-44 or 12:41-44

R. *Praise the Lord, my soul!*

The Lord keeps faith forever,
  executes justice for the oppressed,
  gives food to the hungry.
The Lord sets the prisoners free.

The Lord opens the eyes of the blind.
The Lord lifts up those who are bowed down;
  the Lord loves the righteous.
The Lord watches over the strangers.

He upholds the orphan and the widow,
  but the way of the wicked he brings to ruin.
The Lord will reign forever,
  your God, O Zion, for all generations.
Praise the Lord!

Psalm 146 was used previously this year, on the Twenty-Third Sunday of the Year.

It is the poor widow who appears today: this woman who could give only two small copper coins to the treasury is contrasted with the members of the crowd who ostentatiously contributed large amounts. And the first reading tells the story of a widow who gives all her food to the prophet Elias. Our responsorial song reminds us that the Lord "gives food to the hungry" and supports those in need, both materially and spiritually.

FOR THE JOURNEY

When the local church gathers for worship on Sunday, all its members are called to be present, not only the able-bodied but those with disabilities. When you have a meal, said Jesus, "invite the poor, the maimed, the lame, the blind" (Lk 14:13). In other words, the assembly is not to exclude any of the faithful, no matter what his or her physical condition may be. In fact, with-

112

out the presence of the disabled, the assembly is spiritually diminished because Christ, who underwent the greatest of suffering, is present with them in a special way.

Liturgical ministry is to mirror the assembly, and so the disabled —as their abilities allow—are also to share in this ministry. For example, the visually impaired, using large print Bibles or lectionaries, can be readers.

As to the choir, a disabled person capable of contributing to our ministry should not merely be welcomed into our midst, but should be sought out for membership. His or her presence is a sign of the wholeness of Christ's Body at worship. This presence enriches not only our own sung prayer but also that of the assembly we serve.

ORLAND, INDIANA

Names of saints, churches, biblical places, persons, plants, etc. have all been used to designate hymn tunes. Sometimes composers draw on personal experiences to name the tune.

Naming a tune after a place or a city is not all that unusual. But naming a town after a hymn tune is something else. In the late 1830s a group of settlers in Indiana had a problem in agreeing upon a name for their proposed post office. Someone came up with a solution to the problem. Why not take the singing-school book used by the children and throw it up into the air? Whatever name would appear on the upper half of the left-hand page of the book would be the name of the new town. This was done, the tune was ORLAND, and so it is that there is a small town in Stuben County, Indiana, called Orland.

PRAYER

Lord God,
you fill us with all good things,
with joy, with grace, with love.
Watch over us
as we sing of your wondrous gifts,
as we show our love for you
and for each other
through common song.

"Music, the greatest good that mortals know,
And all of heaven we have below."
Joseph Addison (1672-1719) *Song for St. Cecilia's Day.*

Daniel 12:1-3   Psalm 16:5, 8, 9-10, 11
Hebrews 10:11-14, 18   Mark 13:24-32

R. *Keep me safe, O God;*
  you are my hope.

The Lord is my chosen portion and my cup;
  you hold my lot.
I keep the Lord always before me;
  because he is at my right hand, I shall not be moved.

Therefore my heart is glad, and my soul rejoices;
  my body also rests secure.
For you do not give me up to Sheol,
  or let your faithful one see the Pit.

You show me the path of life.
  In your presence there is fullness of joy;
  in your right hand are pleasures forevermore.

Psalm 16, a psalm of confidence, has two sections: the contrast between Yahweh's faithful ones and those who worship idols (vv. 1-6); the reward given to the person who trusts in God (vv. 7-11).

Today we hear Jesus using the most picturesque language to describe the last day: "the sun will be darkened, the moon will not shed its light." A somewhat similar event is found in Daniel who speaks of a "time unsurpassed in distress." Whenever the "last judgment" comes, whatever form it assumes, we need not fear since we place our trust in God: "keep me safe, O God; you are my hope."

FOR THE JOURNEY

There are many things the Gospels do not tell us about Jesus Christ. Did he smile often? Did he exchange quips with his apostles? Did he ever sit down and just do nothing? What foods did he like? Did he always talk about religion?

On the other hand, there are many things that the Gospels do tell us. Jesus loved to teach. He was patient. He was a poet who

114

knew how to use images like "birds" and "flowers" and "water." He enjoyed good conversation, feasts, meals, friendships. And he liked to surprise people.

There is also something else we know. Jesus could sing. He sang in the synagogue and even immediately before his Passion. "After the psalms had been sung, they left for the Mount of Olives" (Mt 26:30). We don't know whether Jesus, about to suffer and die, was really in the mood for singing, but we do know that he did so.

SING A GLEE

A number of us during college days may have been members of the school's glee club, even though few, I suspect, ever sang a glee.

But if you were a male living in seventeenth- or eighteenth-century England, it would have been quite different since glee singing was the rage. A glee (from the Anglo-Saxon *glíw* or *gléo* meaning "entertainment" or " music") was a simple part song, with a secular text, and for unaccompanied male voices. So popular was glee singing that societies were formed to promote this type of music, e.g., the Noblemen's and Gentlemen's Catch Club.

In the U.S. male college choruses, often called glee clubs (e.g., the Harvard Glee Club, the Yale Glee Club), were originally connected with instrumental groups (banjos, mandolins) and performed pieces of an "entertainment" kind. But in the first quarter of the present century these choral organizations began to sing more serious types of music. Eventually the term glee club was often applied to school choral groups having both male and female singers

---

PRAYER

God our Father,
you lead us as we journey to your kingdom.
Give light to our eyes,
strength to our hearts,
and joy to our lips
so that one day we may join our song
to that of all the angels and saints in heaven.

"Solemnities are vain, words are empty, music a waste of time, prayer useless and rites nothing but lies, if they are not transfigured by justice and mercy." Joseph Gelineau, *The Liturgy Today and Tomorrow* (1978).

Daniel 7:13-14   Psalm 93:1, 1-2, 5
Revalation 1:5-8   John 18:33-37

R. *The Lord is king;*
   he is robed in majesty.

The Lord is king, he is robed in majesty;
   the Lord is robed, he is girded with strength.

He has established the world;
   it shall never be moved;
your throne is established from of old;
   you are from everlasting.

Your decrees are very sure;
   holiness befits your house,
   O Lord, forever more.

Psalm 93 is a hymn praising the Lord's kingdom.

One of Christianity's favorite representations of Christ is that of the ruler, the king. Today Jesus speaks of himself as a king whose "kingdom does not belong to this world." In the first reading Daniel presents the "son of man" as receiving "dominion, glory, and kingship; nations and prophets of every language serve him." Although each age must discover for itself the precise form Christ's kingship is to assume, it remains true that "the Lord is king."

FOR THE JOURNEY

It has been said that the church not only has a past, it also has a memory. And so the church takes delight in recalling those men and women who, down through the centuries, have given steadfast witness to Christ.

During the age of the persecutions the faithful gathered on the anniversary day of a martyr's death at his or her tomb in order to celebrate the eucharist. These martyrs (witnesses) were the first to be recognized as official saints, an honor eventually extended to ascetics, virgins, bishops, and others. For centuries each local church or community "canonized" its own saints.

And yet this link with one's forebears not only incorporated the spiritual "giants" of the community but also included all who, to use an ancient expression, had "fallen asleep in the Lord." From the earliest centuries Christians prayed for the dead and sang psalms and hymns in their memory.

Would we not do well—at least sometime during the year—to remember in a special way those who once were members of our choir but who are now part of God's choir above? They continue to sing with us.

FEAST OF CHRIST THE KING

"Christ's peace through Christ's reign" was the motto of Pope Pius XI. So it was that Pius XI in 1925 introduced this feast which was to be celebrated on the last Sunday of October (the post-Vatican II reform of the church calendar placed it on this last Sunday of the year).

This is one of the "didactic" observances in the church year. As the pope said in his encyclical issued at the time, the feast was to be a vehicle for spiritual teaching; it was to be an antidote for what the pope saw as the secularism and naturalism permeating society.

Today's solemnity should not be considered as dreaming for the re-establishment of that medieval Christendom when all Europe could be considered "Christian," when rulers, officials, teachers, and all society were members of one religious body. Today's celebration is much more extensive in purpose: it looks to the time when Christ will come in all his glory to establish the fullness of his kingdom, a kingdom that will embrace all, a kingdom that will surpass both space and time.

PRAYER

Lord God,
your kingdom is one of peace,
of joy, and of love.
Rule our hearts and our lives
so that we may be
faithful singers of your song.

"On a feast-day, time stands still for a moment, restlessness and the stir of business fall back, people 'take their time' . . . A feast implies an exaltation of human existence. Festive clothes and games, above all music and song, characterize a feast-day." Joseph Jungmann, *Pastoral Liturgy* (1960).